The Mahabharata Virata Parva

by

Kisari Mohan Ganguli

Double 9 BOOKS

The Mahabharata Virata Parva
by Kisari Mohan Ganguli

ISBN: 978-93-59326-78-8

Published by

DOUBLE 9 BOOKS
2/13-B, Ansari Road
Daryaganj, New Delhi – 110002
info@double9books.com
www.double9books.com
Tel. 011-40042856

ABOUT THE AUTHOR

Kisari Mohan Ganguli (also known as K. M. Ganguli) was an Indian translator who was the first to produce an English translation of the Sanskrit epic Mahabharata. His translation was published as Krishna-Dwaipayana Vyasa's Mahabharata. Pratap Chandra Roy (1842-1895), a Calcutta bookseller who owned a printing press and donated funding for the project, translated it into English prose between 1883 and 1896. The chain of events that led to the publication is mentioned in the "Translator's Preface" in Book 1: Adi Parva, Ganguli. Sometime in the early 1870s, Pratapa Chandra Roy visited Ganguli at his home in Shibpur, Howrah, Bengal, with Babu Durga Charan Banerjee, requesting that he take up the translation project, which he did after initial reluctance and a second meeting, when extensive plans were drawn, and a copy of a translation by Max Müller was left behind, which Ganguli found to be literal and lacking in flow. As a result, he began altering the text line by line, "without compromising faithfulness to the original." Soon after, a dozen sheets of his first 'copy' were typed and sent to notable writers, both European and Indian, and it wasn't until they responded positively that the initiative was launched.

CONTENTS

SECTION I 9

SECTION II 11

SECTION III 13

SECTION IV 15

SECTION V 19

SECTION VI 21

SECTION VII 24

SECTION VIII 26

SECTION IX 28

SECTION X 31

SECTION XI 33

SECTION XII 35

SECTION XIII 37

SECTION XIV 40

SECTION XV 44

SECTION XVI 46

SECTION XVII 49

SECTION XVIII 51

SECTION XIX 53
SECTION XX 56
SECTION XXI 58
SECTION XXII 61
SECTION XXII 66
SECTION XXIV 68
SECTION XXV 70
SECTION XXVI 72
SECTION XXVII 74
SECTION XXVIII 75
SECTION XXIX 78
SECTION XXX 79
SECTION XXXI 81
SECTION XXXII 83
SECTION XXXIII 85
SECTION XXXIV 89
SECTION XXXV 91
SECTION XXXVI 93
SECTION XXXVII 95
SECTION XXXVIII 98
SECTION XXXIX 101
SECTION XL 103
SECTION XLI 104

SECTION XLII 105

SECTION XLIII 106

SECTION XLIV 108

SECTION XLV 110

SECTION XLVI 113

SECTION XLVII 115

SECTION XLVIII 117

SECTION XLIX 119

SECTION L 121

SECTION LI 123

SECTION LII 125

SECTION LIII 127

SECTION LIV 129

SECTION LV 132

SECTION LVI 136

SECTION LVII 138

SECTION LVIII 141

SECTION LIX 145

SECTION LX 147

SECTION LXI 149

SECTION LXII 152

SECTION LXIII 154

SECTION LXIV 157

SECTION LXV 159

SECTION LXVI 162

SECTION LXVII 164

SECTION LXVIII 168

SECTION LXIX 170

SECTION LXX 172

SECTION LXXI 174

SECTION LXXII 177

SECTION I

(Pandava-Pravesa Parva)

OM! Having bowed down to Narayana, and Nara, the most exalted of male beings, and also to the goddess Saraswati, must the word *Jaya* be uttered.

Janamejaya said, "How did my great-grandfathers, afflicted with the fear of Duryodhana, pass their days undiscovered in the city of Virata? And, O Brahman, how did the highly blessed Draupadi, stricken with woe, devoted to her lords, and ever adoring the Deity 1 , spend her days unrecognised?"

Vaisampayana said, "Listen, O lord of men, how thy great grandfathers passed the period of unrecognition in the city of Virata. Having in this way obtained boons from the god of Justice, that best of virtuous men, Yudhishthira, returned to the asylum and related unto the Brahmanas all that had happened. And having related everything unto them, Yudhishthira restored to that regenerate Brahmana who had followed him the churning staff and the fire-sticks he had lost. And, O Bharata, the son of the god of Justice, the royal Yudhishthira of high soul then called together all his younger brothers and addressed them, saying, 'Exiled from our kingdom, we have passed twelve years. The thirteenth year, hard to spend, hath now come. Do thou therefore, O Arjuna, the son of Kunti, select some spot where we may pass our days undiscovered by our enemies.'

"Arjuna replied, "Even by virtue of Dharma's boon, we shall, O lord of men, range about undiscovered by men. Still, for purposes of residence, I shall mention some spots that are both delightful and secluded. Do thou select some one of them. Surrounding the kingdom of the Kurus, are, many countries beautiful and abounding in corn, such as Panchala, Chedi, Matsya, Surasena, Pattachchara, Dasarna, Navarashtra, Malla, Salva, Yugandhara, Saurashtra, Avanti, and the spacious Kuntirashtra. Which of these, O king, wouldst thou choose, and where, O foremost of monarchs, shall we spend this year?'

"Yudhishthira said 'O thou of mighty arms, it is even so. What that adorable Lord of all creatures hath said must become true. Surely, after consulting together, we must select some delightful, auspicious, and agreeable region for our abode, where we may live free from fear. The aged Virata, king of the Matsyas, is virtuous and powerful and charitable, and is liked by all. And he is also attached to the Pandavas. Even in the city of Virata, O child, we shall, O Bharata, spend this year, entering his service. Tell me, ye sons of the Kuru race, in what capacities ye will severally present yourselves before the king of the Matsyas!'

"Arjuna said, 'O god among men, what service wilt thou take in Virata's kingdom? O righteous one, in what capacity wilt thou reside in the city of Virata? Thou art mild, and charitable, and modest, and virtuous, and firm in promise. What wilt thou, O king, afflicted as thou art with calamity, do? A king is qualified to bear trouble like an ordinary person. How wilt thou overcome this great calamity that has overtaken thee?'

"Yudhishthira replied, 'Ye sons of the Kuru race, ye bulls among men, hear what I shall do on appearing before king Virata. Presenting myself as a Brahmana, Kanka by name, skilled in dice and fond of play, I shall become a courtier of that high-souled king. And moving upon chess-boards beautiful pawns made of ivory, of blue and yellow and red and white hue, by throws of black and red dice, I shall entertain the king with his courtiers and friends. And while I shall continue to thus delight the king, nobody will succeed in discovering me. And should the monarch ask me, I shall say, *Formerly I was the bosom friend of Yudhishthira.* I tell you that it is thus that I shall pass my days (in the city of Virata). What office wilt thou, O Vrikodara, fill in the city of Virata?'"

SECTION II

"Bhima said, 'I intend to present myself before the lord of Virata as a cook bearing the name of Vallava. I am skilled in culinary art, and I shall prepare curries for the king, and excelling all those skilful cooks that had hitherto dressed his food I shall gratify the monarch. And I shall carry mighty loads of wood. And witnessing that mighty feat, the monarch will be pleased. And, O Bharata, beholding such superhuman feats of mine, the servants of the royal household will honour me as a king. And I shall have entire control over all kinds of viands and drinks. And commanded to subdue powerful elephants and mighty bulls, I will do as bidden. And if any combatants will fight with me in the lists, then will I vanquish them, and thereby entertain the monarch. But I shall not take the life of any of them. I shall only bring them down in such way that they may not be killed. And on being asked as regards my antecedent I shall say that—*Formerly I was the wrestler and cook of Yudhishthira.* Thus shall I, O king, maintain myself.'

"Yudhishthira said, 'And what office will be performed by that mighty descendant of the Kurus, Dhananjaya, the son of Kunti, that foremost of men possessed of long arms, invincible in fight, and before whom, while he was staying with Krishna, the divine Agni himself desirous of consuming the forest of Khandava had formerly appeared in the guise of a Brahmana? What office will be performed by that best of warriors, Arjuna, who proceeded to that forest and gratified Agni, vanquishing on a single car and slaying huge *Nagas* and *Rakshasas*, and who married the sister of Vasuki himself, the king of the *Nagas*? Even as the sun is the foremost of all heat-giving bodies, as the Brahmana is the best of all bipeds, as the cobra is the foremost of all serpents, as Fire is the first of all things possessed of energy, as the thunderbolt is the foremost of all weapons, as the humped bull is the foremost of all animals of the bovine breed, as the ocean is the foremost of all watery expanses, as clouds charged with rain are the foremost of all clouds, as Ananta is the first of all *Nagas*, as Airavata is the foremost of all elephants, as the son is the foremost of all beloved objects, and lastly, as the wife is the best of all friends, so, O Vrikodara, is the youthful Gudakesa, the foremost of all bowmen. And O Bharata, what office will be performed by Vibhatsu, the wielder of *Gandiva*, whose car is drawn by white horses, and who is not inferior to Indra or Vasudeva Himself? What office will be performed by Arjuna who, dwelling for five years in the abode of the thousand-eyed Deity (Indra) shining in celestial lustre, acquired by his own energy the science of superhuman arms with all celestial weapons, and whom I regard as the tenth *Rudra,* the thirteenth *Aditya,* the ninth *Vasu,* and the tenth *Graha,* whose arms, symmetrical and long, have the skin hardened by constant strokes of the bowstring and cicatrices which resemble those on the humps of bulls,—that foremost of warriors who is as Himavat among mountains, the ocean among expanses of water, Sakra among the celestial, Havyavaha (fire) among the Vasus, the tiger among beasts, and Garuda among feathery tribes!'

"Arjuna replied, 'O lord of the Earth, I will declare myself as one of the neuter sex. O monarch, it is, indeed difficult to hide the marks of the bowstring on my arms. I will, however, cover both my cicatrized arms with bangles. Wearing brilliant rings on my ears and conch-bangles on my wrists and causing a braid to hang down from my head, I shall, O king, appear as one of the third sex, Vrihannala by name. And living as a female I shall (always) entertain the king and the inmates of the inner apartments by reciting stories. And, O king, I shall also instruct the women of Virata's palace in singing and delightful modes of dancing and in musical instruments of diverse kinds. And I shall also recite the various excellent acts of men and thus conceal myself, O son of Kunti, by feigning disguise. And, O Bharata should the king enquire, I will say that, *I lived as a waiting maid of Draupadi in Yudhishthira's palace.* And, O foremost of kings, concealing myself by this means, as fire is concealed by ashes, I shall pass my days agreeably in the palace of Virata.'"

Vaisampayana continued, "Having said this, Arjuna, that best of men and foremost of virtuous persons, became silent. Then the king addressed another brother of his." 2

SECTION III

"Yudhishthira said, 'Tender, possessed of a graceful presence, and deserving of every luxury as thou art, what office wilt thou, O heroic Nakula, discharge while living in the dominions of that king? Tell me all about it!'

"Nakula said, 'Under the name of Granthika, I shall become the keeper of the horses of king Virata. I have a thorough knowledge (of this work) and am skilful in tending horses. Besides, the task is agreeable to me, and I possess great skill in training and treating horses; and horses are ever dear to me as they are to thee, O king of the Kurus. At my hands even colts and mares become docile; these never become vicious in bearing a rider or drawing a car. 3 And those persons in the city of Virata that may enquire of me, I shall, O bull of the Bharata race, say,—*Formerly I was employed by Yudhishthira in the charge of his horses*. Thus disguised, O king, I shall spend my days delightfully in the city of Virata. No one will be able to discover me as I will gratify the monarch thus!' 4

"Yudhishthira said, 'How wilt thou, O Sahadeva, bear thyself before that king? And what, O child, is that which thou wilt do in order to live in disguise.'

"Sahadeva replied, 'I will become a keeper of the king of Virata's kine. I am skilled in milking kine and taking their history as well as in taming their fierceness. Passing under the name of Tantripala, I shall perform my duties deftly. Let thy heart's fever be dispelled. Formerly I was frequently employed to look after thy kine, and, O Lord of earth, I have a particular knowledge of that work. And, O monarch, I am well-acquainted with the nature of kine, as also with their auspicious marks and other matters relating to them. I can also discriminate bulls with auspicious marks, the scent of whose urine may make even the barren being forth child. Even thus will I live, and I always take delight in work of this kind. Indeed, no one will then be able to recognise me, and I will moreover gratify the monarch.'

"Yudhishthira said, 'This is our beloved wife dearer to us than our lives. Verily, she deserveth to be cherished by us like a mother, and regarded like an elder sister. Unacquainted as she is with any kind of womanly work, what office will Krishna, the daughter of Drupada, perform? Delicate and young, she is a princess of great repute. Devoted to her lords, and eminently virtuous, also, how will she live? Since her birth, she hath enjoyed only garlands and perfumes and ornaments and costly robes.'

"Draupadi replied, 'There is a class of persons called *Sairindhris,* 5 who enter the services of other. Other females, however (that are respectable) do not do so. Of this class there are some. I shall give myself out as a *Sairindhri,* skilled in dressing hair. And, O Bharata, on being questioned by the king, I shall say that I served as a waiting woman of Draupadi in Yudhishthira's household. I shall thus pass my days in disguise. And I shall serve the famous Sudeshna, the wife of the king. Surely, obtaining me she will cherish me (duly). Do not grieve so, O king.'

"Yudhishthira said, 'O Krishna, thou speakest well. But O fair girl, thou wert born in a respectable family. Chaste as thou art, and always engaged in observing virtuous vows, thou knowest not what is sin. Do thou, therefore, conduct thyself in such a way that sinful men of evil hearts may not be gladdened by gazing at thee.'"

SECTION IV

"Yudhishthira said, 'Ye have already said what offices ye will respectively perform. I also, according to the measure of my sense, have said what office I will perform. Let our priest, accompanied by charioteers and cooks, repair to the abode of Drupada, and there maintain our *Agnihotra* fires. And let Indrasena and the others, taking with them the empty cars, speedily proceeded to Dwaravati. Even this is my wish. And let all these maid-servants of Draupadi go to the Panchalas, with our charioteers and cooks. And let all of them say,—*We do not know where the Pandavas have gone leaving us at the lake of Dwaitavana*.'"

Vaisampayana said, "Having thus taken counsel of one another and told one another the offices they would discharge, the Pandavas sought Dhaumya's advice. And Dhaumya also gave them advice in the following words, saying, 'Ye sons of Pandu, the arrangements ye have made regarding the Brahmanas, your friends, cars, weapons, and the (sacred) fires, are excellent. But it behoveth thee, O Yudhishthira, and Arjuna specially, to make provision for the protection of Draupadi. Ye king, ye are well-acquainted with the characters of men. Yet whatever may be your knowledge, friends may from affection be permitted to repeat what is already known. Even this is subservient to the eternal interests of virtue, pleasure, and profit. I shall, therefore speak to you something. Mark ye. To dwell with a king is, alas, difficult. I shall tell you, ye princes, how ye may reside in the royal household, avoiding every fault. Ye Kauravas, honourably or otherwise, ye will have to pass this year in the king's palace, undiscovered by those that know you. Then in the fourteenth year, ye will live happy. O son of Pandu, in this world, that cherisher and protector of all beings, the king, who is a deity in an embodied form, is as a great fire sanctified with all the *mantras*. 6 One should present himself before the king, after having obtained his permission at the gate. No one should keep contact with royal secrets. Nor should one desire a seat which another may covet. He who doth not, regarding himself to be a favourite, occupy (the king's) car, or coach, or seat, or vehicle, or elephant, is alone worthy of dwelling in a royal household. He that sits not upon a seat the occupation of which is calculated raise alarm in the minds of malicious people, is alone worthy of dwelling in a royal household. No one should, unasked offer counsel (to a king). Paying homage in season unto the king, one should silently and respectfully sit beside the king, for kings take umbrage at babblers, and disgrace lying counsellors. A wise person should not contact friendship with the king's wife, nor with the inmates of the inner apartments, nor with those that are objects of royal displeasure. One about the king should do even the most unimportant acts and with the king's knowledge. Behaving thus with a sovereign, one doth not come by harm. Even if an individual attain the highest office, he should, as long as he is not asked or commanded, consider himself as born-blind, having regard to the king's dignity, for O repressers of foes, the rulers of men do not forgive even their sons and grandsons and brothers when they happen to tamper with their dignity. Kings should be served with regardful care, even as Agni and other gods; and he that is disloyal to his sovereign, is certainly destroyed by him. Renouncing anger, and pride, and negligence, it behoveth a man to follow the course directed by the monarch. After carefully deliberating on all things, a person should set forth before the king those topics that are both profitable and pleasant; but should a subject be profitable without being pleasant, he should still communicate it, despite its disagreeableness. It behoveth a man to be well-disposed towards the king in all his interests, and not to indulge in speech that is alike unpleasant and profitless. Always thinking—*I am not liked by the king*—one should banish negligence, and be intent on bringing about what is agreeable and advantageous to him. He that swerveth not from his place, he that is not friendly to those that are hostile to the king, he that striveth not to do wrong to the king, is alone worthy to dwell in a royal household. A learned man should sit either on the king's right or the left; he should not sit behind him for that is the place appointed for armed guards, and to sit before him is always interdicted. Let none, when the king is engaged in doing anything (in respect of his servants) come forward pressing himself zealously before others, for even if the aggrieved be very poor, such conduct would still be inexcusable. 7 It behoveth no man to reveal to others any lie the king may have told inasmuch as the king bears ill will to those that report his falsehoods. Kings also always disregard persons that regard themselves as learned. No man should be proud thinking—*I am brave, or, I am intelligent*, but a person obtains the good graces of a king and enjoys the good things of life, by behaving agreeably to the wishes of the king. And, O Bharata, obtaining things agreeable, and wealth also which is so hard to acquire, a person should always do what is profitable as well as pleasant to the king. What man that is respected by the wise can even think of doing mischief to one whose ire is great impediment and whose favour is productive of mighty fruits? No one should move his lips, arms and thighs, before the king. A person should speak and spit before the king only mildly. In the presence of even laughable objects, a man should not break out into loud laughter, like a maniac; nor should one show (unreasonable) gravity by containing himself, to the utmost. One should smile modestly, to show his interest (in what is before him). He that is ever mindful of the king's welfare, and is neither exhilarated by reward nor depressed by disgrace, is alone worthy of dwelling in a royal household. That learned courtier who always pleaseth the king and his son with agreeable speeches, succeedeth in dwelling in a royal household as a favourite. The favourite courtier who, having lost the royal favour for just reason, does not speak evil of the king, regains prosperity. The man who serveth the king or liveth in his domains, if sagacious, should speak in praise of the king, both in his presence and absence. The courtier who attempts to obtain his end by employing force on the king, cannot keep his place long and incurs also the risk of death. None should, for the purpose of self-interest, open communications with the king's enemies. 8 Nor should one distinguish himself above the king in matters requiring ability and talents. He that is always cheerful and strong, brave and truthful and mild, and of subdued senses, and who followeth his master like his shadow, is alone worthy to dwell in a royal household. He that on being entrusted with a work, cometh forward, saying,—*I will do this*—is alone worthy of living in a royal household. He that on being entrusted with a task, either within the king's dominion or out of it, never feareth to undertake it, is alone fit to reside in a royal household. He that living away from his home, doth no remember his dear ones, and who undergoeth (present) misery in expectation of (future) happiness, is alone worthy of dwelling in a royal household. One should not dress like the king, nor should one indulge in laughter in the king's presence nor should one disclose royal secrets. By acting thus one may win royal favour. Commissioned to a task, one should not touch bribes for by such appropriation one becometh liable to fetters or death. The robes, ornaments, cars, and other things which the king may be pleased to bestow should always be used, for by this, one winneth the royal favour. Ye children, controlling your minds, do ye spend this year, ye sons of Pandu, behaving in this way. Regaining your own kingdom, ye may live as ye please.'

"Yudhishthira said, 'We have been well taught by thee. Blessed be thou. There is none that could say so to us, save our mother Kunti and Vidura of great wisdom. It behoveth thee to do all that is necessary now for our departure, and for enabling us to come safely through this woe, as well as for our victory over the foe.'"

Vaisampayana continued, "Thus addressed by Yudhishthira, Dhaumya, that best of Brahmanas, performed according to the ordinance the rites ordained in respect of departure. And lighting up their fires, he offered, with *mantras*, oblations on them for the prosperity and success of the Pandavas, as for their reconquest of the whole world. And walking round those fires and round the Brahmanas of ascetic wealth, the six set out, placing Yajnaseni in their front. And when those heroes had departed, Dhaumya, that best of ascetics, taking their sacred fires, set out for the Panchalas. And Indrasena, and others already mentioned, went to the Yadavas, and looking after the horses and the cars of the Pandavas passed their time happily and in privacy."

SECTION V

Vaisampayana said, "Girding their waists with swords, and equipped with finger-protectors made of iguana skins and with various weapons, those heroes proceeded in the direction of the river Yamuna. And those bowmen desirous of (speedily) recovering their kingdom, hitherto living in inaccessible hills and forest fastnesses, now terminated their forest-life and proceeded to the southern bank of that river. And those mighty warriors endued with great strength and hitherto leading the lives of hunters by killing the deer of the forest, passed through *Yakrilloma* and Surasena, leaving behind, on their right, the country of the Panchalas, and on their left, that of the Dasarnas. And those bowmen, looking wan and wearing beards and equipped with swords, entered Matsya's dominions leaving the forest, giving themselves out as hunters. And on arriving at that country, Krishna addressed Yudhishthira, saying, 'We see footpaths here, and various fields. From this it appears that Virata's metropolis is still at a distance. Pass we here what part of the night is still left, for great is my fatigue.'

"Yudhishthira answered, 'O Dhananjaya of Bharata's race, do thou take up Panchali and carry her. Just on emerging from this forest, we arrive at the city.'"

Vaisampayana continued, "Thereupon like the leader of a herd of elephants, Arjuna speedily took up Draupadi, and on coming to the vicinity of the city, let her down. And on reaching the city, Ruru's son (Yudhishthira), addressed Arjuna, saying, 'Where shall we deposit our weapons, before entering the city? If, O child, we enter it with our weapons about us, we shall thereby surely excite the alarm of the citizens. Further, the tremendous bow, the *Gandiva*, is known to all men, so that people will, without doubt, recognise us soon. And if even one of us is discovered, we shall, according to promise, have to pass another twelve years in the forest.'

"Arjuna said, 'Hard by yon cemetery and near that inaccessible peak is a mighty *Sami* tree, throwing-about its gigantic branches and difficult to ascend. Nor is there any human being, who, I think, O Pandu's son, will espy us depositing our arms at that place. That tree is in the midst of an out-of-the way forest abounding in beasts and snakes, and is in the vicinity of a dreary cemetery. Stowing away our weapons on the *Sami* tree, let us, O Bharata, go to the city, and live there, free from anxiety!'"

Vaisampayana continued, "Having O bull of the Bharata race spoken thus to king Yudhishthira the just, Arjuna prepared to deposit the weapons (on the tree). And that bull among the Kurus, then loosened the string of the large and dreadful *Gandiva*, ever producing thundering twang and always destructive of hostile hosts, and with which he had conquered, on a single car, gods and men and *Nagas* and swelling provinces. And the warlike Yudhishthira, that represser of foes, unfastened the undecaying string of that bow with which he had defended the field of Kurukshetra. And the illustrious Bhimasena unstrung that bow by means of which that sinless one had vanquished in fight the Panchalas and the lord of Sindhu, and with which, during his career of conquest, he had, single-handed, opposed innumerable foes, and hearing whose twang which was like unto the roar of the thunder or the splitting of a mountain, enemies always fly (in panic) from the field of battle. And that son of Pandu of coppery complexion and mild speech who is endued with great prowess in the field, and is called Nakula in consequence of his unexampled beauty in the family, then unfastened the string of that bow with which he had conquered all the regions of the west. And the heroic Sahadeva also, possessed of a mild disposition, then untied the string of that bow with which he had subjugated the countries of the south. And with their bows, they put together their long and flashing swords, their precious quivers, and their arrows sharp as razors. And Nakula ascended the tree, and deposited on it the bows and the other weapons. And he tied them fast on those parts of the tree which he thought would not break, and where the rain would not penetrate. And the Pandavas hung up a corpse (on the tree), knowing that people smelling the stench of the corpse would say—*here sure, is a dead body*, and avoid the tree from a distance. And on being asked by the shepherds and cowherds regarding the corpse, those repressers of foes said unto them, 'This is our mother, aged one hundred and eighty years. We have hung up her dead body, in accordance with the custom observed by our forefathers.' And then those resisters of foes approached the city. And for purposes of non-discovery Yudhishthira kept these (five) names for himself and his brothers respectively, viz., Jaya, Jayanta, Vijaya, Jayatsena, and Jayadvala. Then they entered the great city, with the view to passing the thirteenth year undiscovered in that kingdom, agreeably to the promise (to Duryodhana)."

SECTION VI

Vaisampayana said, "And while Yudhishthira was on his way to the delightful city of Virata, he began to praise mentally the Divine Durga, the Supreme Goddess of the Universe, born on the womb of Yasoda, and fond of the boons bestowed on her by Narayana, sprung from the race of cowherd Nanda, and the giver of prosperity, the enhancer (of the glory) of (the worshipper's) family, the terrifier of Kansa, and the destroyer of *Asuras,*—and saluted the Goddess—her who ascended the skies when dashed (by Kansa) on a stony platform, who is the sister of Vasudeva, one who is always decked in celestial garlands and attired in celestial robes,—who is armed with scimitar and shield, and always rescues the worshipper sunk in sin, like a cow in the mire, who in the hours of distress calls upon that eternal giver of blessings for relieving him of their burdens. And the king, desirous with his brothers of obtaining a sight of the Goddess, invoked her and began to praise her by reciting various names derived from (approved) hymns. And Yudhishthira said, 'Salutations to thee, O giver of boons. O thou that art identical with Krishna, O maiden, O thou that hast observed the vow of *Brahmacharya,* O thou of body bright as the newly-risen Sun, O thou of face beautiful as the full moon. Salutations to thee, O thou of four hands and four faces, O thou of fair round hips and deep bosom, O thou that wearest bangles made of emeralds and sapphires, O thou that bearest excellent bracelets on thy upper arm. Thou shinest, O Goddess, as Padma, the consort of Narayana. O thou that rangest the etherial regions, thy true form and thy *Brahmacharya* are both of the purest kind. Sable as the black clouds, thy face is beautiful as that of *Sankarshana.* Thou bearest two large arms long as a couple of poles raised in honour of Indra. In thy (six) other arms thou bearest a vessel, a lotus, a bell, a noose, a bow, a large discus, and various other weapons. Thou art the only female in the universe that possessest the attribute of purity. Thou art decked with a pair of well-made ears graced with excellent rings. O Goddess, thou shinest with a face that challengeth the moon in beauty. With an excellent diadem and beautiful braid with robes made of the bodies of snakes, and with also the brilliant girdle round thy hips, thou shinest like the Mandara mountain encircled with snakes. Thou shinest also with peacock-plumes standing erect on thy head, and thou hast sanctified the celestial regions by adopting the vow of perpetual maiden-hood. It is for this, O thou that hast slain the *Mahishasura*,[9] that thou art praised and worshipped by the gods for the protection of the three worlds. O thou foremost of all deities, extend to me thy grace, show me thy mercy, and be thou the source of blessings to me. Thou art *Jaya* and *Vijaya*, and it is thou that givest victory in battle. Grant me victory, O Goddess, and give me boons also at this hour of distress. Thy eternal abode is on Vindhya—that foremost of mountains. O *Kali*, O *Kali*, thou art the great *Kali*, ever fond of wine and meat and animal sacrifice. Capable of going everywhere at will, and bestowing boons on thy devotees, thou art ever followed in thy journeys by Brahma and the other gods. By them that call upon thee for the relief of their burdens, and by them also that bow to thee at daybreak on Earth, there is nothing that cannot be attained in respect either of offspring or wealth. And because thou rescuest people from difficulties whether when they are afflicted in the wilderness or sinking in the great ocean, it is for this that thou art called *Durga*[10] by all. Thou art the sole refuge of men when attacked by robbers or while afflicted in crossing streams and seas or in wilderness and forests. Those men that remember thee are never prostrated, O great Goddess. Thou art Fame, thou art Prosperity, thou art Steadiness, thou art Success; thou art the Wife, thou art men's Offspring, thou art Knowledge, and thou art the Intellect. Thou art the two Twilights, the Night Sleep, Light—both solar and lunar, Beauty, Forgiveness, Mercy, and every other thing. Thou dispellest, worshipped by the devotees their fetters, ignorance, loss of children and loss of wealth, disease, death, and fear. I, who have been deprived of my kingdom, seek thy protection. And as I bow to thee with bended head, O Supreme Goddess, grant me protection, O thou of eyes like lotus leaves. And be thou as boon-giving Truth unto us that are acting according to Truth. And, O Durga, kind as thou art unto all that seek thy protection, and affectionate unto all thy devotees, grant me protection!'"

Vaisampayana continued, "Thus praised by the son of Pandu, the Goddess showed herself unto him. And approaching the king, she addressed him in these words, 'O mighty armed king, listen, O Lord, to these words of mine. Having vanquished and slain the ranks of the Kauravas through my grace, victory in battle will soon be thine. Thou shalt again lord it over the entire Earth, having made thy dominions destitute of thorns. And, O king, thou shalt also, with thy brothers, obtain great happiness. And through my grace, joy and health will be thine. And they also in the world who will recite my attributes and achievements will be freed from their sins, and gratified. I will bestow upon them kingdom, long life, beauty of person, and offspring. And they, O king, who will invoke me, after thy manner, in exile or in the city, in the midst of battle or of dangers from foes, in forests or in inaccessible deserts, in seas or mountain fastnesses, there is nothing that they will not obtain in this world. And ye sons of Pandu, he will achieve success in every business of his that will listen to, or himself recite with devotion, this excellent hymn. And through my grace neither the Kuru's spies, nor those that dwell in the country of the Matsyas, will succeed in recognising you all as long as ye reside in Virata's city!' And having said these words unto Yudhishthira, that chastiser of foes, and having arranged for the protection of the sons of Pandu, the Goddess disappeared there and then."

SECTION VII

Vaisampayana said, "Then tying up in his cloth dice made of gold and set with *lapis lazuli*, and holding them below his arm-pit, king Yudhishthira,—that illustrious lord of men—that high-souled perpetuator of the Kuru race, regarded by kings, irrepressible in might, and like unto a snake of virulent poison,—that bull among men, endued with strength and beauty and prowess, and possessed of greatness, and resembling in form a celestial though now like unto the sun enveloped in dense clouds, or fire covered with ashes, first made his appearance when the famous king Virata was seated in his court. And beholding with his followers that son of Pandu in his court, looking like the moon hid in clouds and possessed of a face beautiful as the full moon, king Virata addressed his counsellors and the twice-born ones and the charioteers and the Vaisyas and others, saying, 'Enquire ye who it is, so like a king that looketh on my court for the first time. He cannot be a Brahmana. Methinks he is a man of men, and a lord of earth. He hath neither slaves, nor cars, nor elephants with him, yet he shineth like the very Indra. The marks on his person indicate him to be one whose coronal locks have undergone the sacred investiture. Even this is my belief. He approacheth me without any hesitation, even as an elephant in rut approacheth an assemblage of lotuses!'

"And as the king was indulging in these thoughts, that bull among men, Yudhishthira, came before Virata and addressed him, saying, 'O great king, know me for a Brahmana who, having lost his all hath come to thee for the means of subsistence. I desire, O sinless one, to live here beside thee acting under thy commands, 11 O lord.' The king then, well-pleased, replied unto him saying, 'Thou art welcome. Do thou then accept the appointment thou seekest!' And having appointed the lion among kings in the post he had prayed for, king Virata addressed him with a glad heart, saying, 'O child, I ask thee from affection, from the dominions of what king dost thou come hither? Tell me also truly what is thy name and family, and what thou hast a knowledge of.'

"Yudhishthira said, 'My name is Kanka, and I am a Brahmana belonging to the family known by the name of *Vaiyaghra*. I am skilled in casting dice, and formerly I was a friend of Yudhishthira.'

"Virata replied, 'I will grant thee whatever boon thou mayst desire. Do thou rule the Matsyas.—I shall remain in submission to thee. Even cunning gamblers are liked by me. Thou, on the other hand, art like a god, and deservest a kingdom.'

"Yudhishthira said, 'My first prayer, O lord of earth, is that I may not be involved in any dispute (on account of dice) with low people. Further, a person defeated by me (at dice) shall not be permitted to retain the wealth (won by me). Let this boon be granted to me through thy grace.'

"Virata replied, 'I shall certainly slay him who may happen to displease thee, and should he be one of the twice-born ones, I shall banish him from my dominions. Let the assembled subjects listen! Kanka is as much lord of this realm as I myself. Thou (Kanka) shalt be my friend and shalt ride the same vehicles as I. And there shall also be at thy disposal apparel in plenty, and various kinds of viands and drinks. And thou shalt look into my affairs, both internal and external. And for thee all my doors shall be open. When men out of employ or of strained circumstances will apply to thee, do thou at all hours bring their words unto me, and I will surely give them whatever they desire. No fear shall be thine as long as thou residest with me.'"

Vaisampayana said, "Having thus obtained an interview with Virata's king, and received from him boons, that heroic bull among men, began to live happily, highly regarded by all. Nor could any one discover him as he lived there."

SECTION VIII

Vaisampayana said, "Then another endued with the dreadful strength and blazing in beauty, approached king Virata, with the playful gait of the lion. And holding in hand a cooking ladle and a spoon, as also an unsheathed sword of sable hue and without a spot on the blade, he came in the guise of a cook illumining all around him by his splendour like the sun discovering the whole world. And attired in black and possessed of the strength of the king of mountains, he approached the king of the Matsyas and stood before him. And beholding that king-like person before him, Virata addressed his assembled subjects saying, 'Who is that youth, that bull among men, with shoulders broad like those of a lion, and so exceedingly beautiful? That person, never seen before, is like the sun. Revolving the matter in my mind, I cannot ascertain who he is, nor can I with even serious thoughts guess the intention of that bull among men (in coming here). Beholding him, it seems to me that he is either the king of the Gandharvas, or Purandara himself. Do ye ascertain who it is that standeth before my eyes. Let him have quickly what he seeks.' Thus commanded by king Virata, his swift-footed messengers went up to the son of Kunti and informed that younger brother of Yudhishthira of everything the king had said. Then the high-souled son of Pandu, approaching Virata, addressed him in words that were not unsuited to his object, saying, 'O foremost of kings, I am a cook, Vallava by name. I am skilled in dressing dishes. Do thou employ me in the kitchen!'

"Virata said, 'I do not believe, O Vallava, that cooking is thy office. Thou resemblest the deity of a thousand eyes; and in grace and beauty and prowess, thou shinest among these all as a king!'

"Bhima replied, 'O king of kings, I am thy cook and servant in the first place. It is not curries only of which I have knowledge, O monarch, although king Yudhishthira always used in days gone by to taste my dishes. O lord of earth, I am also a wrestler. Nor is there one that is equal to me in strength. And engaging in fight with lions and elephants, I shall, O sinless one, always contribute to thy entertainment.'

"Virata said, 'I will even grant thee boons. Thou wilt do what thou wishest, as thou describest thyself skilled in it. I do not, however, think, that this office is worthy of thee, for thou deservest this (entire) earth girt round by the sea. But do as thou likest. Be thou the superintendent of my kitchen, and thou art placed at the head of those who have been appointed there before by me.'"

Vaisampayana continued, "Thus appointed in the kitchen, Bhima soon became the favourite of king Virata. And, O king, he continued to live there unrecognised by the other servants of Virata as also by other people!"

SECTION IX

Vaisampayana said, "Binding her black, soft, fine, long and faultless tresses with crisped ends into a knotted braid, Draupadi of black eyes and sweet smiles, throwing it upon her right shoulders, concealed it by her cloth. And she wore a single piece of a black and dirty though costly cloth. And dressing herself as a *Sairindhri*, she began to wander hither and thither in seeming affliction. And beholding her wandering, men and women came to her hastily and addressed her, saying, 'Who are you? And what do you seek?' And she replied, 'I am a king's *Sairindhri*. I desire to serve any one that will maintain me.' But beholding her beauty and dress, and hearing also her speech that was so sweet, the people could not take her for a maid-servant in search of subsistence. And it came to pass that while looking this way and that from the terrace, Virata's beloved queen, daughter of the king of Kekaya, saw Draupadi. And beholding her forlorn and clad in a single piece of cloth, the queen addressed her saying, 'O beautiful one, who are you, and what do you seek?' Thereupon, Draupadi answered her, saying, 'O foremost of queens, I am *Sairindhri*. I will serve anybody that will maintain me.' Then Sudeshna said, 'What you say (regarding your profession) can never be compatible with so much beauty. (On the contrary) you might well be the mistress of servants both, male and female. Your heels are not prominent, and your thighs touch each other. And your intelligence is great, and your navel deep, and your words solemn. And your great toes, and bust and hips, and back and sides, and toe-nails, and palms are all well-developed. And your palms, soles, and face are ruddy. And your speech is sweet even as the voice of the swan. And your hair is beautiful, and your bust shapely, and you are possessed of the highest grace. And your hips and bust are plump. And like a Kashmerean mare you are furnished with every auspicious mark. And your eye-lashes are (beautiful) bent, and your nether-lip is like the ruddy ground. And your waist is slender, and your neck bears lines that resemble those of the conch. And your veins are scarcely visible. Indeed, your countenance is like the full moon, and your eyes resemble the leaves of the autumnal lotus, and your body is fragrant as the lotus itself. Verily, in beauty you resemble *Sri* herself, whose seat is the autumnal lotus. Tell me, O beautiful damsel, who thou art. Thou canst never be a maidservant. Art thou a *Yakshi*, a Goddess, a *Gandharvi*, or an *Apsara*? Art thou the daughter of a celestial, or art thou a female *Naga*? Art thou the guardian goddess of some city, a *Vidyadhari*, or a *Kinnari*,—or art thou *Rohini* herself? Or art thou Alamvusha, or Misrakesi, Pundarika, or Malini, or the queen of Indra, or of Varuna? Or, art thou the spouse of Viswakarma, or of the creative Lord himself? Of these goddesses who art renowned in the celestial regions, who art thou, O graceful one?'

"Draupadi replied, 'O auspicious lady, I am neither a goddess nor a *Gandharvi*, nor a *Yakshi*, nor a *Rakshasi*. I am a maid-servant of the *Sairindhri* class. I tell thee this truly. I know to dress the hair, to pound (fragrant substances) for preparing unguents, and also to make beautiful and variegated garlands, O beauteous lady, of jasmines and lotuses and blue lilies and *Champakas*. Formerly I served Krishna's favourite queen Satyabhama, and also Draupadi, the wife of the Pandavas and the foremost beauty of the Kuru race. I wander about alone, earning good food and dress; and as long as I get these, I continue to live in the place where they are obtainable. Draupadi herself called me Malini (maker of garlands).'

"Hearing this, Sudeshna said, 'I would keep thee upon my head itself, if the doubt did not cross my mind that the king himself would be attracted towards thee with his whole heart. Attracted by thy beauty, the females of the royal household and my maids are looking at thee. What male person then is there that can resist thy attraction? Surely, O thou of well-rounded hips, O damsel of exquisite charms, beholding thy form of superhuman beauty, king Virata is sure to forsake me, and will turn to thee with his whole heart. O thou of faultless limbs, O thou that art endued with large eyes casting quick glances, he upon whom thou wilt look with desire is sure to be stricken. O thou of sweet smiles, O thou that possessest a faultless form, he that will behold thee constantly, will surely catch the flame. Even as a person that climbs up a tree for compassing his own destruction, even as the crab conceives for her own ruin, I may, O thou of sweet smiles, bring destruction upon myself by harbouring thee.'

"Draupadi replied, 'O fair lady, neither Virata nor any other person will be able to have me, for my five youthful husbands, who are *Gandharvas* and sons of a *Gandharva* king of exceeding power, always protect me. None can do me a wrong. It is the wish of my *Gandharva* husbands that I should serve only such persons as will not give me to touch food already partaken of by another, or tell me to wash their feet. Any man that attempts to have me like any common woman, meeteth with death that very night. No one can succeed in having me, for, O beautiful lady, O thou of sweet smiles, those beloved *Gandharvas*, possessed of great energy and mighty strength always protect me secretly.'

"Sudeshna said, 'O thou that bringest delight to the heart, if it is as thou sayest, I will take thee into my household. Thou shalt not have to touch food that hath been partaken of by another, or to wash another's feet.'"

Vaisampayana continued, "Thus addressed by Virata's wife, O Janamejaya, Krishna (Draupadi) ever devoted to her lords, began to live in that city. Nor could anyone ascertain who in reality she was!"

SECTION X

"Vaisampayana said, 'Then clad in a cowherd's dress, and speaking the dialect of cowherds, Sahadeva came to the cowpen of Virata's city. And beholding that bull among men, who was shining in splendour, the king was struck with amazement. And he directed his men to summon Sahadeva. And when the latter came, the king addressed him, saying, 'To whom dost thou belong? And whence dost thou come? And what work dost thou seek? I have never seen thee before. O bull among men, tell me truly about thee.'

"Having come before the king that afflicter of foes, Sahadeva answered in accents deep as the roar of the cloud, 'I am a Vaisya, Arishtanemi by name. I was employed as a cowherd in the service of those bulls of the Kuru race, the sons of Pandu. O foremost of men, I intend now to live beside thee, for I do not know where those lions among kings, the sons of Pritha, are. I cannot live without service, and, O king, I do not like to enter into the service of anyone else save thee.'

"Hearing these words, Virata said, 'Thou must either be a Brahmana or a Kshatriya. Thou lookest as if thou wert the lord of the entire earth surrounded by the sea. Tell me truly, O thou that mowest down thy foes. The office of a Vaisya is not fit for thee. Tell me from the dominions of what king thou comest, and what thou knowest, and in what capacity thou wouldst remain with us, and also what pay thou wouldst accept.'

"Sahadeva answered, 'Yudhishthira, the eldest of the five sons of Pandu, had one division of kine numbering eight hundred and ten thousand, and another, ten thousand, and another, again, twenty thousand, and so on. I was employed in keeping those cattle. People used to call me Tantripala. I know the present, the past, and the future of all kine living within ten *Yojanas*, and whose *tale* has been taken. My merits were known to that illustrious one, and the Kuru king Yudhishthira was well-pleased with me. I am also acquainted with the means which aid kine in multiplying within a short time, and by which they may enjoy immunity from disease. Also these arts are known to me. I can also single out bulls having auspicious marks for which they are worshipped by men, and by smelling whose urine, the barren may conceive.'

"Virata said, 'I have a hundred thousand kine divided into distinct herds. All those together with their keepers, I place in thy charge. Henceforth my beasts will be in thy keep.'"

Vaisampayana continued, "Then, O king, undiscovered by that monarch, that lord of men, Sahadeva, maintained by Virata, began to live happily. Nor did anyone else (besides his brothers) recognise him."

SECTION XI

"Vaisampayana said, 'Next appeared at the gate of the ramparts another person of enormous size and exquisite beauty decked in the ornaments of women, and wearing large ear-rings and beautiful conch-bracelets overlaid with gold. And that mighty-armed individual with long and abundant hair floating about his neck, resembled an elephant in gait. And shaking the very earth with his tread, he approached Virata and stood in his court. And beholding the son of the great Indra, shining with exquisite lustre and having the gait of a mighty elephant,—that grinder of foes having his true form concealed in disguise, entering the council-hall and advancing towards the monarch, the king addressed all his courtiers, saying, 'Whence doth this person come? I have never heard of him before.' And when the men present spoke of the newcomer as one unknown to them, the king wonderingly said, 'Possessed of great strength, thou art like unto a celestial, and young and of darkish hue, thou resemblest the leader of a herd of elephants. Wearing conch-bracelets overlaid with gold, a braid, and ear-rings, thou shinest yet like one amongst those that riding on chariots wander about equipped with mail and bow and arrows and decked with garlands and fine hair. I am old and desirous of relinquishing my burden. Be thou like my son, or rule thou like myself all the Matsyas. It seemeth to me that such a person as thou can never be of the neuter sex.'

"Arjuna said, 'I sing, dance, and play on instruments. I am proficient in dance and skilled in song. O lord of men, assign me unto (the princess) Uttara. I shall be dancing-master to the royal maiden. As to how I have come by this form, what will it avail thee to hear the account which will only augment my pain? Know me, O king of men, to be Vrihannala, a son or daughter without father or mother.'

"Virata said, 'O Vrihannala, I give thee what thou desirest. Instruct my daughter, and those like her, in dancing. To me, however, this office seemeth unworthy of thee. Thou deservest (the dominion of) the entire earth girt round by the ocean.'"

Vaisampayana continued, "The king of the Matsyas then tested Vrihannala in dancing, music, and other fine arts, and consulting with his various ministers forthwith caused him to be examined by women. And learning that this impotency was of a permanent nature, he sent him to the maiden's apartments. And there the mighty Arjuna began giving lessons in singing and instrumental music to the daughter of Virata, her friends, and her waiting-maids, and soon won their good graces. And in this manner the self-possessed Arjuna lived there in disguise, partaking of pleasures in their company, and unknown to the people within or without the palace."

SECTION XII

Vaisampayana said, "After a while, another powerful son of Pandu was seen making towards king Virata in haste. And as he advanced, he seemed to everyone like solar orb emerged from the clouds. And he began to observe the horses around. And seeing this, the king of the Matsyas said to his followers, 'I wonder whence this man, possessed of the effulgence of a celestial, cometh. He looks intently at my steeds. Verily, he must be proficient in horse-lore. Let him be ushered into my presence quickly. He is a warrior and looks like a god!' And that destroyer of foes then went up to the king and accosted him, saying, 'Victory to thee, O king, and blest be ye. As a trainer of horses, I have always been highly esteemed by kings. I will be a clever keeper of thy horses.'

"Virata said, 'I will give thee vehicles, wealth, and spacious quarters. Thou shalt be the manager of my horses. But first tell me whence thou comest, who thou art, and how also thou happenest to come here. Tell us also all the arts thou art master of.' Nakula replied, 'O mower of enemies, know that Yudhishthira is the eldest brother of the five sons of Pandu. I was formerly employed by him to keep his horses. I am acquainted with the temper of steeds, and know perfectly the art of breaking them. I know also how to correct vicious horses, and all the methods of treating their diseases. No animal in my hands becometh weak or ill. Not to speak of horses, even mares in my hands will never be found to be vicious. People called me Granthika by name and so did Yudhishthira, the son of Pandu.'

"Virata said, 'Whatever horses I have, I consign to thy care even from today. And all the keepers of my horses and all my charioteers will from today be subordinate to thee. If this suits thee, say what remuneration is desired by thee. But, O thou that resemblest a celestial, the office of equerry is not worthy of thee. For thou lookest like a king and I esteem thee much. The appearance here hath pleased me as much as if Yudhishthira himself were here. Oh, how does that blameless son of Pandu dwell and divert himself in the forest, now destitute of servants as he is.'"

Vaisampayana continued, "That youth, like unto a chief of the *Gandharvas*, was treated thus respectfully by the delighted king Virata. And he conducted himself there in such a manner as to make himself dear and agreeable to all in the palace. And no one recognised him while living under Virata's protection. And it was in this manner then the sons of Pandu, the very sight of whom had never been fruitless, continued to live in the country of the Matsyas. And true to their pledge those lords of the earth bounded by her belt of seas passed their days of *incognito* with great composure notwithstanding their poignant sufferings."

SECTION XIII

(Samayapalana Parva)

Janamejaya said, "While living thus disguised in the city of the Matsyas, what did those descendants of the Kuru race endued with great prowess, do, O regenerate one!"

Vaisampayana said, "Hear, O king, what those descendants of Kuru did while they dwelt thus in disguise in the city of the Matsyas, worshipping the king thereof. By the grace of the sage Trinavindu and of the high-souled lord of justice, the Pandavas continued to live unrecognised by others in the city of Virata. O lord of men, Yudhishthira, as courtier made himself agreeable to Virata and his sons as also to all the Matsyas. An adept in the mysteries of dice, the son of Pandu caused them to play at dice according to his pleasure and made them sit together in the dice-hall like a row of birds bound in a string. And that tiger among men, king Yudhishthira the Just, unknown to the monarch, distributed among his brothers, in due proportion, the wealth he won from Virata. And Bhimasena on his part, sold to Yudhishthira for price, meat and viands of various kinds which he obtained from the king. And Arjuna distributed among all his brothers the proceeds of worn-out cloths which he earned in the inner apartments of the palace. And Sahadeva, too, who was disguised as a cowherd gave milk, curds and clarified butter to his brothers. And Nakula also shared with his brothers the wealth the king gave him, satisfied with his management of the horses. And Draupadi, herself in a pitiable condition, looked after all those brothers and behaved in such a way as to remain unrecognized. And thus ministering unto one another's wants, those mighty warriors lived in the capital of Virata as hidden from view, as if they were once more in their mother's womb. And those lords of men, the sons of Pandu, apprehensive of danger from the son of Dhritarashtra, continued to dwell there in concealment, watching over their wife Draupadi. And after three months had passed away, in the fourth, the grand festival in honour of the divine Brahma which was celebrated with pomp in the country of the Matsyas, came off. And there came athletes from all quarters by thousands, like hosts of celestials to the abode of Brahma or of Siva to witness that festival. And they were endued with huge bodies and great prowess, like the demons called *Kalakhanjas*. And elated with their prowess and proud of their strength, they were highly honoured by the king. And their shoulders and waists and necks were like those of lions, and their bodies were very clean, and their hearts were quite at ease. And they had many a time won success in the lists in the presence of kings. And amongst them there was one who towered above the rest and challenged them all to a combat. And there was none that dared to approach him as he proudly stalked in the arena. And when all the athletes stood sad and dispirited, the king of the Matsyas made him fight with his cook. And urged by the king, Bhima made up his mind reluctantly, for he could not openly disobey the royal behest. And that tiger among men then having worshipped the king, entered the spacious arena, pacing with the careless steps of a tiger. And the son of Kunti then girded up his loins to the great delight of the spectators. And Bhima then summoned to the combat that athlete known by the name of Jimuta who was like unto the Asura Vritra whose prowess was widely known. And both of them were possessed of great courage, and both were endued with terrible prowess. And they were like a couple of infuriate and huge-bodied elephants, each sixty years old. And those brave tigers among men then cheerfully engaged in a wrestling combat, desirous of vanquishing each other. And terrible was the encounter that took place between them, like the clash of the thunderbolt against the stony mountain-breast. And both of them were exceedingly powerful and extremely delighted at each other's strength. And desirous of vanquishing each other, each stood eager to take advantage of his adversary's lapse. And both were greatly delighted and both looked like infuriate elephants of prodigious size. And various were the modes of attack and defence that they exhibited with their clenched fists. 12 And each dashed against the other and flung his adversary to a distance. And each cast the other down and pressed him close to the ground. And each got up again and squeezed the other in his arms. And each threw the other violently off his place by boxing him on the breast. And each caught the other by the legs and whirling him round threw him down on the ground. And they slapped each other with their palms that struck as hard as the thunderbolt. And they also struck each other with their outstretched fingers, and stretching them out like spears thrust the nails into each other's body. And they gave each other violent kicks. And they struck knee and head against head, producing the crash of one stone against another. And in this manner that furious combat between those warriors raged on without weapons, sustained mainly by the power of their arms and their physical and mental energy, to the infinite delight of the concourse of spectators. And all people, O king, took deep interest in that encounter of those powerful wrestlers who fought like Indra and the Asura Vritra. And they cheered both of them with loud acclamations of applause. And the broad-chested and long-armed experts in wrestling then pulled and pressed and whirled and hurled down each other and struck each other with their knees, expressing all the while their scorn for each other in loud voices. And they began to fight with their bare arms in this way, which were like spiked maces of iron. And at last the powerful and mighty-armed Bhima, the slayer of his foes, shouting aloud seized the vociferous athlete by the arms even as the lion seizes the elephant, and taking him up from the ground and holding him aloft, began to whirl him round, to the great astonishment of the assembled athletes and the people of Matsya. And having whirled him round and round a hundred times till he was insensible, the strong-armed Vrikodara dashed him to death on the ground. And when the brave and renowned Jimuta was thus killed, Virata and his friends were filled with great delight. And in the exuberance of his joy, the noble-minded king rewarded Vallava then and there with the liberality of Kuvera. And killing numerous athletes and many other men possessed of great bodily strength, he pleased the king very much. And when no one could be found there to encounter him in the lists, the king made him fight with tigers and lions and elephants. And the king also made him battle with furious and powerful lions in the harem for the pleasure of the ladies. And Arjuna, too, pleased the king and all the ladies of the inner apartments by singing and dancing. And Nakula pleased Virata, that best of kings, by showing him fleet and well-trained steeds that followed him wherever he went. And the king, gratified with him, rewarded him with ample presents. And beholding around Sahadeva a herd of well-trained bullocks, Virata that bull among men, bestowed upon him also wealth of diverse kinds. And, O king, Draupadi distressed to see all those warriors suffer pain, sighed incessantly. And it was in this way that those eminent persons lived there in disguise, rendering services unto king Virata."

SECTION XIV

(Kichaka-badha Parva)

Vaisampayana said, "Living in such disguise, those mighty warriors, the sons of Pritha, passed ten months in Matsya's city. And, O monarch, although herself deserving to be waited upon by others, the daughter of Yajnasena, O Janamejaya, passed her days in extreme misery, waiting upon Sudeshna. And residing thus in Sudeshna's apartments, the princess of Panchala pleased that lady as also the other females of the inner apartments. And it came to pass that as the year was about to expire, the redoubtable Kichaka, the Commander of Virata's forces, chanced to behold the daughter of Drupada. And beholding that lady endued with the splendour of a daughter of the celestials, treading the earth like a goddess, Kichaka, afflicted with the shafts of Kama, desired to possess her. And burning with desire's flame, Virata's general came to Sudeshna (his sister) and smilingly addressed her in these words, 'This beauteous lady had never before been seen by me in king Virata's abode. This damsel maddens me with her beauty, even as a new wine maddens one with its fragrance. Tell me, who is this graceful and captivating lady possessed of the beauty of a goddess, and whose she is, and whence she hath come. Surely, grinding my heart she hath reduced me to subjection. It seems to me that (save her) there is no other medicine for my illness. O, this fair hand-maid of thine seemeth to me to be possessed of the beauty of a goddess. Surely, one like her is ill suited to serve thee. Let her rule over me and whatever is mine. O, let her grace my spacious and beautiful palace, decked with various ornaments of gold, full of viands and drinks in profusion, with excellent plates, and containing every kind of plenty, besides elephants and horses and cars in myriads.' And having consulted with Sudeshna thus, Kichaka went to princess Draupadi, and like a jackal in the forest accosting a lioness, spoke unto Krishna these words in a winning voice, 'Who and whose art thou, O beautiful one? And O thou of beautiful face, whence hast thou come to the city of Virata? Tell me all this, O fair lady. Thy beauty and gracefulness are of the very first order and the comeliness of thy features is unparalleled. With its loveliness thy face shineth ever like the resplendent moon. O thou of fair eye-brows, thy eyes are beautiful and large like lotus-petals. Thy speech also, O thou of beautiful limbs, resembles the notes of the *cuckoo*. O thou of fair hips, never before in this world have I beheld a woman possessed of beauty like thine, O thou of faultless features. Art thou Lakshmi herself having her abode in the midst of lotuses or, art thou, O slender-waisted one, she who is called *Bhuti* 13 . Or, which amongst these—*Hri, Sri, Kirti* and *Kanti,*—art thou, O thou of beautiful face? Or possessed of beauty like Rati's, art thou, she who sporteth in the embraces of the God of love? O thou that possessest the fairest of eye-brows, thou shinest beautifully even like the lovely light of the moon. Who is there in the whole world that will not succumb to the influence of desire beholding thy face? Endued with unrivalled beauty and celestial grace of the most attractive kind, that face of thine is even like the full moon, its celestial effulgence resembling his radiant face, its smile resembling his soft-light, and its eye-lashes looking like the spokes on his disc. Both thy bosoms, so beautiful and well-developed and endued with unrivalled gracefulness and deep and well-rounded and without any space between them, are certainly worthy of being decked with garlands of gold. Resembling in shape the beautiful buds of the lotus, these thy breasts, O thou of fair eye-brows, are even as the whips of Kama that are urging me forward, O thou of sweet smiles. O damsel of slender waist, beholding that waist of thine marked with four wrinkles and measuring but a span, and slightly stooping forward because of the weight of thy breasts, and also looking on those graceful hips of thine broad as the banks of a river, the incurable fever of desire, O beauteous lady, afflicteth me sore. The flaming fire of desire, fierce as a forest conflagration, and fanned by the hope my heart cherisheth of a union with thee is consuming me intensely. O thou of exceeding beauty quench thou that flaming fire kindled by Manmatha. Union with thee is a rain-charged cloud, and the surrender of thy person is the shower that the cloud may drop. O thou of face resembling the moon, the fierce and maddening shafts of Manmatha whetted and sharpened by the desire of a union with thee, piercing this heart of mine in their impetuous course, have penetrated into its core. O black-eyed lady, those impetuous and cruel shafts are maddening me beyond endurance. It behoveth thee to relieve me from this plight by surrendering thyself to me and favouring me with thy embraces. Decked in beautiful garlands and robes and adorned with every ornament, sport thou, O sweet damsel, with me to thy fill. O thou of the gait of an elephant in rut, deserving as thou art of happiness though deprived of it now, it behoveth thee not to dwell here in misery. Let unrivalled weal be thine. Drinking various kinds of charming and delicious and ambrosial wines, and sporting at thy pleasure in the enjoyment of diverse objects of delight, do thou, O blessed lady, attain auspicious prosperity. This beauty of thine and this prime of thy youth, O sweet lady, are now without their use. For, O beauteous and chaste damsel, endued with such loveliness, thou dost not shine, like a graceful garland lying unused and unworn. I will forsake all my old wives. Let them, O thou of sweet smiles, become thy slaves. And I also, O fair damsel, will stay by thee as thy slave, ever obedient to thee, O thou of the most handsome face.' Hearing these words of his, Draupadi replied, 'In desiring me, a female servant of low extraction, employed in the despicable office of dressing hair, O *Suta's* son, thou desirest one that deserves not that honour. Then, again, I am the wife of others. Therefore, good betide thee, this conduct of thine is not proper. Do thou remember the precept of morality, viz., that persons should take delight only in their wedded wives. Thou shouldst not, therefore, by any means bend thy heart to adultery. Surely abstaining from improper acts is ever the study of those that are good. Overcome by ignorance sinful men under the influence of desire come by either extreme infamy or dreadful calamity.'"

Vaisampayana continued, "Thus addressed by the *Sairindhri*, the wicked Kichaka losing control over his senses and overcome by lust, although aware of the numerous evils of fornication, evils condemned by everybody and sometimes leading to the destruction of life itself,—then spoke unto Draupadi, 'It behoveth thee not, O beauteous lady, O thou of graceful features, thus to disregard me who am, O thou of sweet smiles, under the power of Manmatha on thy account. If now, O timid one, thou disregardest me who am under thy influence and who speak to thee so fair, thou wilt, O black-eyed damsel, have to repent for it afterwards. O thou of graceful eye-brows, the real lord of this entire kingdom, O slender-waisted lady, is myself. It is me depending upon whom the people of this realm live. In energy and prowess I am unrivalled on earth. There is no other man on earth who rivals me in beauty of person, in youth, in prosperity, and in the possession of excellent objects of enjoyment. Why it is, O auspicious lady, that having it in thy power to enjoy here every object of desire and every luxury and comfort without its equal, thou preferest servitude. Becoming the mistress of this kingdom which I shall confer on thee, O thou of fair face, accept me, and enjoy, O beauteous one, all excellent objects of desire.' Addressed in these accursed words by Kichaka, that chaste daughter of Drupada answered him thus reprovingly, 'Do not, O son of a *Suta*, act so foolishly and do not throw away thy life. Know that I am protected by my five husbands. Thou canst not have me. I have Gandharvas for my husbands. Enraged they will slay thee. Therefore, do thou not bring destruction on thyself. Thou intendest to tread along a path that is incapable of being trod by men. Thou, O wicked one, art even like a foolish child that standing on one shore of the ocean intends to cross over to the other. Even if thou enterest into the interior of the earth, or soarest into the sky, or rushest to the other shore of the ocean, still thou wilt have no escape from the hands of those sky-ranging offspring of gods, capable of grinding all foes. Why dost thou today, O Kichaka, solicit me so persistently even as a sick person wisheth for the night that will put a stop to his existence? Why dost thou desire me, even like an infant lying on its mother's lap wishing to catch the moon? For thee that thus solicitest their beloved wife, there is no refuge either on earth or in sky. O Kichaka, hast thou no sense which leads thee to seek thy good and by which thy life may be saved?'"

SECTION XV

Vaisampayana said, "Rejected thus by the princess, Kichaka, afflicted with maddening lust and forgetting all sense of propriety, addressed Sudeshna saying, 'Do thou, Kekaya's daughter, so act that thy *Sairindhri* may come into my arms. Do thou, O Sudeshna, adopt the means by which the damsel of the gait of an elephant may accept me; I am dying of absorbing desire.'"

Vaisampayana continued, "Hearing his profuse lamentations, that gentle lady, the intelligent queen of Virata, was touched with pity. And having taken counsel with her own self and reflected on Kichaka's purpose and on the anxiety of Krishna, Sudeshna addressed the *Suta's* son in these words, 'Do thou, on the occasion of some festival, procure viands and wines for me. I shall then send my *Sairindhri* to thee on the pretence of bringing wine. And when she will repair thither do thou in solitude, free from interruption, humour her as thou likest. Thus soothed, she may incline her mind to thee.'"

Vaisampayana continued, "Thus addressed, he went out of his sister's apartments. And he soon procured wines well-filtered and worthy of a king. And employing skilled cooks, he prepared many and various kinds of choice viands and delicious drinks and many and various kinds of meat of different degrees of excellence. And when all this had been done, that gentle lady Sudeshna, as previously counselled by Kichaka, desired her *Sairindhri* to repair to Kichaka's abode, saying, 'Get up, O *Sairindhri* and repair to Kichaka's abode to bring wine, for, O beauteous lady, I am afflicted with thirst.' Thereupon the *Sairindhri* replied, 'O princess, I shall not be able to repair to Kichaka's apartments. Thou thyself knowest, O queen, how shameless he is. O thou of faultless limbs, O beauteous lady, in thy palace I shall not be able to lead a lustful life, becoming faithless to my husbands. Thou rememberest, O gentle lady, O beautiful one, the conditions I had set down before entering thy house. O thou of tresses ending in graceful curls, the foolish Kichaka afflicted by the god of desire, will, on seeing me, offer me insult. Therefore, I will not go to his quarters. Thou hast, O princess, many maids under thee. Do thou, good betide thee, send one of them. For, surely, Kichaka will insult me.' Sudeshna said, 'Sent by me, from my abode, surely he will not harm thee.' And having said this, she handed over a golden vessel furnished with a cover. And filled with apprehension, and weeping, Draupadi mentally prayed for the protection of the gods, and set out for Kichaka's abode for fetching wine. And she said, 'As I do not know another person save my husbands, by virtue of that Truth let Kichaka not be able to overpower me although I may approach his presence.'"

Vaisampayana continued, "And that helpless damsel then adored Surya for a moment. And Surya, having considered all that she urged, commanded a *Rakshasa* to protect her invisibly. And from that time the *Rakshasa* began to attend upon that blameless lady under any circumstances. And beholding Krishna in his presence like a frightened doe, the *Suta* rose up from his seat, and felt the joy that is felt by a person wishing to cross to the other shore, when he obtains a boat."

SECTION XVI

"Kichaka said, 'O thou of tresses ending in beautiful curls, thou art welcome. Surely, the night that is gone hath brought me an auspicious day, for I have got thee today as the mistress of my house. Do what is agreeable to me. Let golden chains, and conchs and bright ear-rings made of gold, manufactured in various countries, and beautiful rubies and gems, and silken robes and deer-skins, be brought for thee. I have also an excellent bed prepared for thee. Come, sitting upon it do thou drink with me the wine prepared from the honey flower.' Hearing these words, Draupadi said, 'I have been sent to thee by the princess for taking away wine. Do thou speedily bring me wine, for she told me that she is exceedingly thirsty.' At this, Kichaka said, 'O gentle lady, others will carry what the princess wants.' And saying this, the *Suta's* son caught hold of Draupadi's right arm. And at this, Draupadi exclaimed, 'As I have never, from intoxication of the senses, been unfaithful to my husbands even at heart, by that Truth, O wretch, I shall behold thee dragged and lying powerless on the ground.'"

Vaisampayana continued, "Seeing that large-eyed lady reproving him in that strain, Kichaka suddenly seized her by the end of her upper garment as she attempted to run away. And seized with violence by Kichaka, the beautiful princess, unable to tolerate it, and with frame trembling with wrath, and breathing quickly, dashed him to the ground. And dashed to the ground thus, the sinful wretch tumbled down like a tree whose roots had been cut. And having thrown Kichaka down on the ground when the latter had seized her, she, trembling all over rushed to the court, where king Yudhishthira was, for protection. And while she was running with all her speed, Kichaka (who followed her), seizing her by the hair, and bringing her down on the ground, kicked her in the very presence of the king. Thereupon, O Bharata, the *Rakshasa* that had been appointed by Surya to protect Draupadi, gave Kichaka a shove with a force mighty as that of the wind. And overpowered by the force of *Rakshasa*, Kichaka reeled and fell down senseless on the ground, even like an uprooted tree. And both Yudhishthira and Bhimasena who were seated there, beheld with wrathful eyes that outrage on Krishna by Kichaka. And desirous of compassing the destruction of the wicked Kichaka, the illustrious Bhima gnashed his teeth in rage. And his forehead was covered with sweat, and terrible wrinkles appeared thereon. And a smoky exhalation shot forth from his eyes, and his eye-lashes stood on end. And that slayer of hostile heroes pressed his forehead with his hands. And impelled by rage, he was on the point of starting up with speed. Thereat king Yudhishthira, apprehensive of discovery, squeezed his thumbs and commanded Bhima to forbear. And Bhima who then looked like an infuriate elephant eyeing a large tree, was thus forbidden by his elder brother. And the latter said, 'Lookest thou, O cook, for trees for fuel. If thou art in need of faggots, then go out and fell trees.' And the weeping Draupadi of fair hips, approaching the entrance of the court, and seeing her melancholy lords, desirous yet of keeping up the disguise duty-bound by their pledge, with eyes burning in fire, spoke these words unto the king of the Matsyas, 'Alas, the son of a *Suta* hath kicked today the proud and beloved wife of those whose foe can never sleep in peace even if four kingdoms intervene between him and them. Alas, the son of a *Suta* hath kicked today the proud and beloved wife of those truthful personages, who are devoted to Brahmanas and who always give away without asking any thing in gift. Alas! the son of a *Suta* hath kicked today the proud and beloved wife of those, the sounds of whose kettle-drums and the twangs of whose bow-strings are ceaselessly heard. Alas, the son of a *Suta* hath kicked today the proud and beloved wife of those who are possessed of abundant energy and might, and who are liberal in gifts and proud of their dignity. Alas, the son of a *Suta* hath kicked today the proud and beloved wife of those who, if they had not been fettered by the ties of duty, could destroy this entire world. Where, alas, are those mighty warriors today who, though living in disguise, have always granted protection unto those that solicit it? Oh, why do those heroes today, endued as they are with strength and possessed of immeasurable energy, quietly suffer, like eunuchs, their dear and chaste wife to be thus insulted by a *Suta's* son? Oh, where is that wrath of theirs, that prowess, and that energy, when they quietly bear their wife to be thus insulted by a wicked wretch? What can I (a weak woman) do when Virata, deficient in virtue, coolly suffereth my innocent self to be thus wronged by a wretch? Thou dost not, O king, act like a king towards this Kichaka. Thy behaviour is like that of a robber, and doth not shine in a court. That I should thus be insulted in thy very presence, O Matsya, is highly improper. Oh, let all the courtiers here look at this violence of Kichaka. Kichaka is ignorant of duty and morality, and Matsya also is equally so. These courtiers also that wait upon such a king are destitute of virtue.'"

Vaisampayana continued, "With these and other words of the same kind the beautiful Krishna with tearful eyes rebuked the king of the Matsyas. And hearing her, Virata said, 'I do not know what your dispute has been out of our sight. Not knowing the true cause how can I show my discrimination?' Then the courtiers, having learnt every thing, applauded Krishna, and they all exclaimed, 'Well done!' 'Well done!' and censured Kichaka. And the courtiers said, 'That person who owneth this large-eyed lady having every limb of hers endued with beauty for his wife, possesseth what is of exceeding value and hath no occasion to indulge in any grief. Surely, such a damsel of transcendent beauty and limbs perfectly faultless is rare among men. Indeed, it seems to us that she is a goddess.'"

Vaisampayana continued, "And while the courtiers, having beheld Krishna (under such circumstances), were applauding her thus, Yudhishthira's forehead, from ire, became covered with sweat. And that bull of the Kuru race then addressed that princess, his beloved spouse, saying, 'Stay not here, O Sairindhri; but retire to the apartments of Sudeshna. The wives of heroes bear affliction for the sake of their husbands, and undergoing toil in ministering unto their lords, they at last attain to region where their husbands may go. Thy Gandharva husbands, effulgent as the sun, do not, I imagine, consider this as an occasion for manifesting their wrath, inasmuch as they do not rush to thy aid. O *Sairindhri*, thou art ignorant of the timeliness of things, and it is for this that thou weepest as an actress, besides interrupting the play of dice in Matsya's court. Retire, O *Sairindhri*; the Gandharvas will do what is agreeable to thee. And they will surely display thy woe and take the life of him that hath wronged thee.' Hearing these words the *Sairindhri* replied, 'They of whom I am the wedded wife are, I ween, extremely kind. And as the eldest of them all is addicted to dice, they are liable to be oppressed by all.'"

Vaisampayana continued, "And having said this, the fair-hipped Krishna with dishevelled hair and eyes red in anger, ran towards the apartments of Sudeshna. And in consequence of having wept long her face looked beautiful like the lunar disc in the firmament, emerged from the clouds. And beholding her in that condition, Sudeshna asked, 'Who, O beauteous lady, hath insulted thee? Why, O amiable damsel, dost thou weep? Who, gentle one, hath done thee wrong? Whence is this thy grief?' Thus addressed, Draupadi said, 'As I went to bring wine for thee, Kichaka struck me in the court in the very presence of the king, as if in the midst of a solitary wood.' Hearing this, Sudeshna said, 'O thou of tresses ending in beautiful curls, as Kichaka, maddened by lust hath insulted thee that art incapable of being possessed by him, I shall cause him to be slain if thou wishest it.' Thereupon Draupadi answered, 'Even others will slay him,—even they whom he hath wronged. I think it is clear that he will have to go to the abode of Yama this very day!'"

SECTION XVII

Vaisampayana said, "Thus insulted by the *Suta's* son, that illustrious princess, the beautiful Krishna, eagerly wishing for the destruction of Virata's general, went to her quarters. And Drupada's daughter of dark hue and slender waist then performed her ablutions. And washing her body and cloths with water Krishna began to ponder weepingly on the means of dispelling her grief. And she reflected, saying, 'What am I to do? Whither shall I go? How can my purpose be effected?' And while she was thinking thus, she remembered Bhima and said to herself, 'There is none else, save Bhima, that can today accomplish the purpose on which my heart is set!' And afflicted with great grief, the large-eyed and intelligent Krishna possessed of powerful protectors then rose up at night, and leaving her bed speedily proceeded towards the quarters of Bhimasena, desirous of beholding her lord. And possessed of great intelligence, the daughter of Drupada entered her husband's quarters, saying, 'How canst thou sleep while that wretched commander of Virata's forces, who is my foe, yet liveth, having perpetrated today *that* (foul act)?'"

Vaisampayana continued, "Then the chamber where Bhima slept, breathing hard like a lion, being filled with the beauty of Drupada's daughter and of the high-souled Bhima, blazed forth in splendour. And Krishna of sweet smiles, finding Bhimasena in the cooking apartments, approached him with the eagerness of a three-year old cow brought up in the woods, approaching a powerful bull, in her first season, or of a she-crane living by the water-side approaching her mate in the pairing season. And the Princess of Panchala then embraced the second son of Pandu, even as a creeper embraces a huge and mighty *Sala* on the banks of the Gomati. And embracing him with her arms, Krishna of faultless features awaked him as a lioness awaketh a sleeping lion in a trackless forest. And embracing Bhimasena even as a she-elephant embraceth her mighty mate, the faultless Panchali addressed him in voice sweet as the sound of a stringed instrument emitting *Gandhara* note. And she said, 'Arise, arise! Why dost thou, O Bhimasena, lie down as one dead? Surely, he that is not dead, never suffereth a wicked wretch that hath disgraced his wife, to live.'

And awakened by the princess, Bhima of mighty arms, then rose up, and sat upon his couch overlaid with a rich bed. And he of the Kuru race then addressed the princess—his beloved wife, saying, 'For what purpose hast thou come hither in such a hurry? Thy colour is gone and thou lookest lean and pale. Tell me everything in detail. I must know the truth. Whether it be pleasurable or painful, agreeable, or disagreeable, tell me all. Having heard everything, I shall apply the remedy. I alone, O Krishna, am entitled to thy confidence in all things, for it is I who deliver thee from perils again and again! Tell me quickly what is thy wish, and what is the purpose that is in thy view, and return thou to thy bed before others awake.'"

SECTION XVIII

"Draupadi said, 'What grief hath she not who hath Yudhishthira for her husband? Knowing all my griefs, why dost thou ask me? The *Pratikamin* dragged me to the court in the midst of an assembly of courtiers, calling me a slave. That grief, O Bharata, consumeth me. What other princess, save Draupadi, would live having suffered such intense misery? Who else, save myself, could bear such second insult as the wicked Saindhava offered me while residing in the forest? Who else of my position, save myself, could live, having been kicked by Kichaka in the very sight of the wicked king of the Matsyas? Of what value is life, O Bharata, when thou, O son of Kunti, dost not think me miserable, although I am afflicted with such woes? That vile and wicked wretch, O Bharata, known by the name of Kichaka, who is the brother-in-law of king Virata and the commander of his forces, every day, O tiger among men, addresses me who am residing in the palace as a *Sairindhri*, saying, *Do thou become my wife.*—Thus solicited, O slayer of foes, by that wretch deserving to be slain, my heart is bursting like a fruit ripened in season. Censure thou that elder brother of thine addicted to execrable dice, through whose act alone I have been afflicted with such woe. Who else, save him that is a desperate gambler, would play, giving up kingdom and everything including even myself, in order to lead a life in the woods? If he had gambled morning and evening for many years together, staking *nishkas* by thousand and other kinds of substantial wealth, still his silver, and gold, and robes, and vehicles, and teams, and goats, and sheep, and multitudes of steeds and mares and mules would not have sustained any diminution. But now deprived of prosperity by the rivalry of dice, he sits dumb like a fool, reflecting on his own misdeeds. Alas, he who, while sojourning, was followed by ten thousand elephants adorned with golden garlands now supports himself by casting dice. That Yudhishthira who at Indraprastha was adored by kings of incomparable prowess by hundreds of thousands, that mighty monarch in whose kitchen a hundred thousand maid-servants, plate in hand, used every day to feed numerous guests day and night, that best of liberal men, who gave (every day) a thousand *nishkas*, alas, even he overwhelmed with woe in consequence of gambling which is the root of all evil, now supporteth himself by casting dice. Bards and encomiasts by thousands decked with ear-rings set with brilliant gems, and gifted with melodious voice, used to pay him homage morning and evening. Alas, that Yudhishthira, who was daily waited upon by a thousand sages of ascetic merit, versed in the *Vedas* and having every desire gratified, as his courtiers,—that Yudhishthira who maintained eighty-eight thousands of domestic *Snatakas* with thirty maid-servants assigned unto each, as also ten thousand *yatis* not accepting anything in gift and with vital seed drawn up,—alas, even that mighty king now liveth in such guise. That Yudhishthira who is without malice, who is full of kindness, and who giveth every creature his due, who hath all these excellent attributes, alas—even he now liveth in such guise. Possessed of firmness and unbaffled prowess, with heart disposed to give every creature his due, king Yudhishthira, moved by compassion, constantly maintained in his kingdom the blind, the old, the helpless, the parentless and all others in his dominions in such distress. Alas, that Yudhishthira becoming a dependant and a servant of Matsya, a caster of dice in his court, now calls himself Kanka. He unto whom while residing at Indraprastha, all the rulers of earth used to pay timely tribute,—alas, even he now begs for subsistence at another's hands. He to whom the kings of the earth were in subjection,—alas, even that king having lost his liberty, liveth in subjection to others. Having dazzled the entire earth like the sun by his energy, that Yudhishthira, alas, is now a courtier of king Virata. O Pandu's son, that Pandava who was respectfully waited upon in court by kings and sages, behold him now waiting upon another. Alas, beholding Yudhishthira a courtier sitting beside another and breathing adulatory speeches to the other, who can help being afflicted with grief? And beholding the highly wise and virtuous Yudhishthira, undeserving as he is of serving others, actually serving another for sustenance, who can help being afflicted with grief? And, O hero, that Bharata who was worshipped in court by the entire earth, do thou now behold him worshipping another. Why then, O Bharata, dost thou not regard me as one afflicted with diverse miseries, like one forlorn and immersed in a sea of sorrow?'"

SECTION XIX

"Draupadi said, 'This O Bharata, that I am going to tell thee is another great grief of mine. Thou shouldst not blame me, for I tell thee this from sadness of heart. Who is there whose grief is not enhanced at sight of thee, O bull of the Bharata race, engaged in the ignoble office of a cook, so entirely beneath thee and calling thyself as one *of Vallava* caste? What can be sadder than this, that people should know thee as Virata's cook, Vallava by name, and therefore one that is sunk in servitude? Alas, when thy work of the kitchen is over, thou humbly sittest beside Virata, calling thyself as Vallava the cook, then despondency seizeth my heart. When the king of kings in joy maketh thee fight with elephants, and the women of the inner apartments (of the palace) laugh all the while, then I am sorely distressed. When thou fightest in the inner apartments with lions, tigers, and buffaloes, the princess Kaikeyi looking on, then I almost swoon away. And when Kaikeyi and those maidservants, leaving their seats, come to assist me and find that instead of suffering any injury in limbs mine is only a swoon, the princess speaks unto her women, saying, 'Surely, it is from affection and the duty begot of intercourse that this lady of sweet smiles grieveth for the exceedingly powerful cook when he fights with the beasts. Sairindhri is possessed of great beauty and Vallava also is eminently handsome. The heart of woman is hard to know, and they, I fancy, are deserving of each other. It is, therefore, likely that the Sairindhri invariably weepeth (at such times) on account of her connection with her lover. And then, they both have entered this royal family at the same time. And speaking such words she always upbraideth me. And beholding me wroth at this, she suspects me to be attached to thee.' When she speaketh thus, great is the grief that I feel. Indeed, on beholding thee, O Bhima of terrible prowess, afflicted with such calamity, sunk as I already am in grief on account of Yudhishthira, I do not desire to live. That youth who on a single car had vanquished all celestials and men, is now, alas, the dancing master of king Virata's daughter. That Pritha's son of immeasurable soul, who had gratified Agni in the forest of Khandava, is now living in the inner apartments (of a palace) like fire hid in a well. Alas, the bull among men, Dhananjaya, who was ever the terror of foes, is now living in a guise that is despaired by all. Alas, he whose mace-like arms have been cicatrized in consequence of the strokes of his bow-string, alas that Dhananjaya is passing the days in grief covering his wrists with bracelets of conchs. Alas, that Dhananjaya the twang of whose bow-string and the sound of whose leathern fences made every foe tremble, now entertains only gladdened women with his songs. Oh, that Dhananjaya whose head was formerly decked with a diadem of solar splendour, is now wearing braids ending in unsightly curls. O Bhima, beholding that terrible bowman, Arjuna, now wearing braids and in the midst of women, my heart is stricken with woe. That high-souled hero who is master of all the celestial weapons, and who is the repository of all the sciences, now weareth ear-rings (like one of the fair sex). That youth whom kings of incomparable prowess could not overpower in fight, even as the waters of the mighty ocean cannot overleap the continents, is now the dancing-master of king Virata's daughters and waits upon them in disguise. O Bhima, that Arjuna the clatter of whose car-wheels caused the entire earth with her mountains and forests, her mobile and immobile things to tremble, and whose birth dispelled all the sorrows of Kunti, that exalted hero, that younger brother of thine, O Bhimasena, now maketh me weep for him. Beholding him coming towards me, decked in golden ear-rings and other ornaments, and wearing on the wrists bracelets of conchs, my heart is afflicted with despondency. And Dhananjaya who hath not a bowman equal unto him on earth in prowess, now passeth his days in singing, surrounded by women. Beholding that son of Pritha who in virtue, heroism and truth, was the most admired in the world, now living in the guise of a woman, my heart is afflicted with sorrow. When I behold, the godlike Partha in the music-hall like an elephant with rent temples surrounded by she-elephants in the midst of females, waiting before Virata the king of the Matsyas, then I lose all sense of directions. Surely, my mother-in-law doth not know Dhananjaya to be afflicted with such extreme distress. Nor doth she know that descendant of the Kuru race, Ajatasatru, addicted to disastrous dice, to be sunk in misery. O Bharata, beholding the youngest of you all, Sahadeva, superintending the kine, in the guise of a cowherd, I grow pale. Always thinking of Sahadeva's plight, I cannot, O Bhimasena, obtain sleep,—what to speak you of the rest? I do not know, O mighty-armed one, what sin Sahadeva may have committed for which that hero of unbaffled prowess suffereth such misery. O foremost of the Bharatas, beholding that beloved brother of thine, that bull among men, employed by Matsya in looking after his kine, I am filled with woe. Seeing that hero of proud disposition gratifying Virata, by living at the head of his cowherds, attired in robes dyed in red, I am attacked with fever. My mother-in-law always applauds the heroic Sahadeva as one possessed of nobility, excellent behaviour, and rectitude of conduct. Ardently attached to her sons, the weeping Kunti stood, embracing Sahadeva while he was about to set out (with us) for the great forest. And she addressed me saying, "Sahadeva is bashful and sweet-speeched, and virtuous. He is also my favourite child. Therefore, O Yajnaseni, tend him in the forest day and night. Delicate and brave, devoted to the king, and always worshipping his elder brother, do thou, O Panchali, feed him thyself." O Pandava, beholding that foremost of warriors, Sahadeva, engaged in tending kine, and sleeping at night on calf-skins, how can I bear to live? He again who is crowned with the three attributes of beauty, arms, and intelligence, is now the superintendent of Virata's steeds. Behold the change brought on by time. Granthika (Nakula), at sight of whom hostile hosts fled from the field of battle, now traineth horses in the presence of the king, driving them with the speed. Alas, I now see that handsome youth wait upon the gorgeously decked and excellent Virata, the king of the Matsyas, and display horses before him. O son of Pritha, afflicted as I am with all these hundred kinds of misery on account of Yudhishthira, why dost thou, O chastiser of foes, yet deem me happy? Listen now to me, O son of Kunti, as I tell thee of other woes far surpassing these. What can be sadder to me than miseries so various as these should emaciate me while ye are alive.'"

SECTION XX

"Draupadi said, 'Alas, on account of that desperate gambler, I am now under Sudeshna's command, living in the palace in the guise of a *Sairindhri*. And, O chastiser of foes, behold the plight of poignant woe which I, a princess, am now in. I am living in expectation of the close of this stated period. 14 The extreme of misery, therefore, is mine. Success of purpose, victory, and defeat, as regards mortals, are transitory. It is in this belief that I am living in expectation of the return of prosperity to my husbands. Prosperity and adversity revolve like a wheel. It is in this belief that I am living in expectation of the return of prosperity to my husbands. That cause which bringeth on victory, may bring defeat as well. I live in this hope. Why dost thou not, O Bhimasena, regard me as one dead? I have heard that persons that give may beg: that they who slay may be slain; and that they who over-throw others may themselves be overthrown by foes. Nothing is difficult for Destiny and none can over-ride Destiny. It is for this that I am awaiting the return of favourable fortune. As a tank once dried, is filled up once again, so hoping for a change for the better, I await the return of prosperity. When one's business that hath been well-provided for is seen to be frustrated, a truly wise person should never strive for bringing back good fortune. Plunged as I am an sorrow, asked or unasked by thee to explain the purpose of these words spoken by me, I shall tell thee everything. Queen of the sons of Pandu and daughter of Drupada, who else, save myself, would wish to live, having fallen into such a plight? O represser of foes, the misery, therefore, that hath overtaken me, hath really humiliated the entire *Kuru* race, the Panchalas, and the sons of Pandu. Surrounded by numerous brothers and father-in-law and sons, what other woman having such cause for joy, save myself, would be afflicted with such woe? Surely, I must, in my childhood, have committed act highly offensive to *Dhatri* through whose displeasure, O bull of the Bharata race, I have been visited with such consequences. Mark, O son of Pandu, the pallour that hath come over my complexion which not even a life in the woods fraught as it was with extreme misery, could bring about. Thou, O Pritha's son, knowest what happiness, O Bhima, was formerly mine. Even I, who was such have now sunk into servitude. Sorely distressed, I can find no rest. That the mighty-armed and terrible bowman, Dhananjaya the son of Pritha, should now live like a fire that hath been put out, maketh me think of all this as attributable to Destiny. Surely, O son of Pritha, it is impossible for men to understand the destinies of creatures (in this world). I, therefore, think this downfall of yours as something that could not be averted by forethought. Alas, she who hath you all, that resemble Indra himself to attend to her comforts—even she, so chaste and exalted, hath now to attend to the comforts of others, that are to her far inferior in rank. Behold, O Pandava, my plight. It is what I do not deserve. You are alive, yet behold this inversion of order that time hath brought. She who had the whole Earth to the verge of the sea under her control, is now under the control of Sudeshna and living in fear of her. She who had dependants to walk both before and behind her, alas, now herself walketh before and behind Sudeshna. This, O Kaunteya, is another grief of mine that is intolerable. O, listen to it. She who had never, save for Kunti, pounded unguents even for her own use, now, good betide thee, poundeth sandal (for others). O Kaunteya, behold these hands of mine which were not so before.' Saying this she showed him her hands marked with corns. And she continued, 'she who had never feared Kunti herself nor thee and thy brothers, now standeth in fear before Virata as a slave, anxious of what that king of kings may say unto her regarding the proper preparation of the unguents, for Matsya liketh not sandal pounded by others.'"

Vaisampayana continued, "Relating her woes thus, O Bharata, unto Bhimasena, Krishna began to weep silently, casting her eyes on Bhima. And then, with words choked in tears, and sighing repeatedly, she addressed Bhima in these words, powerfully stirring his heart, 'Signal, O Bhima, must have been my offence of old unto the gods, for, unfortunate as I am. I am yet alive, when, O Pandava, I should die.'"

Vaisampayana continued, "Then that slayer of hostile heroes, Vrikodara, covering his face with those delicate hands of his wife marked with corns, began to weep. And that mighty son of Kunti, holding the hands of Draupadi in his, shed copious tears. And afflicted with great woe, he spoke these words."

SECTION XXI

"Bhima said, 'Fie on the might of my arms and fie on the *Gandiva* of Phalguna, inasmuch as thy hands, red before, now become covered with corns. I would have caused a carnage in Virata's court but for the fact that Kunti's son eyed me (by way of forbidding it), or like a mighty elephant, I would, without ado, have crushed the head of Kichaka intoxicated with the pride of sovereignty. When, O Krishna, I beheld thee kicked by Kichaka, I conceived at that instant a wholesale slaughter of the Matsyas. Yudhishthira, however, forbade me by a glance, and, O beauteous lady, understanding his intention I have kept quiet. That we have been deprived of our kingdom, that I have not yet slain the Kurus, that I have not yet taken the heads of Suyodhana and Karna, and Suvala's son Sakuni, and the wicked Duhsasana, these acts and omissions, O lady, are consuming every limb of mine. The thought of those abides in my heart like a javelin implanted in it. O thou of graceful hips, do not sacrifice virtue, and, O noble-hearted lady, subdue thy wrath. If king Yudhishthira hear from thee such rebukes, he will surely put an end to his life. If also Dhananjaya and the twins hear thee speak thus, even they will renounce life. And if these, O slender-waisted maiden, give up life, I also shall not be able to bear my own. In olden days Sarjati's daughter, the beautiful Sukanya, followed into the forest Chyavana of Bhrigu's race, whose mind was under complete control, and over whom, while engaged in ascetic meditation, the ants had built a hill. Thou mayst have heard that Indrasena also who in beauty was like unto *Narayani* herself, followed her husband aged a thousand years. Thou mayst have heard that Janaka's daughter Sita, the princess of Videha, followed her lord while living in dense woods. And that lady of graceful hips, Rama's beloved wife, afflicted with calamities and persecuted by the Rakshasas, at length regained the company of Rama. Lopamudra also, O timid one, endued with youth and beauty, followed Agastya, renouncing all the objects of enjoyment unattainable by men. And the intelligent and faultless Savitri also followed the heroic Satyavan, the son of Dyumatsena, alone into the world of Yama. Even like these chaste and beautiful ladies that I have named, thou, O blessed girl, bloomest with every virtue. Do thou spend a short while more that is measured by even a half month. And when the thirteenth year is complete, thou wilt (again) become the Queen regnant of a king.' Hearing these words, Draupadi said, 'Unable, O Bhima, to bear my griefs, it is from grief alone that I have shed these tears. I do not censure Yudhishthira. Nor is there any use in dwelling on the past. O Bhima of mighty strength, come quickly forward to the work of the hour. O Bhima, Kaikeyi, jealous of my beauty, always pains me by her endeavours to prevent the king from taking a fancy to me. And understanding this disposition of hers, the wicked-souled Kichaka of immoral ways constantly solicits me himself. Angry with him for this, but then suppressing my wrath I answer that wretch deprived of sense by lust, saying, "O Kichaka, protect thyself. I am the beloved queen and wife of five Gandharvas. Those heroes in wrath will slay thee that art so rash." Thus addressed, Kichaka of wicked soul replied unto me, saying, "I have not the least fear of the Gandharvas, O Sairindhri of sweet smiles. I will slay hundred thousand Gandharvas, encountering them in battle. Therefore, O timid one, do thou consent." Hearing all this, I again addressed the lust-afflicted Suta, saying, "Thou art no match for those illustrious Gandharvas. Of respectable percentage and good disposition, I ever adhere to virtue and never wish for the death of any one. It is for this that thou I vest, O Kichaka!" At this, that wight of wicked soul burst out into a loud laughter. And it came to pass that Kaikeyi previously urged by Kichaka, and moved by affection for her brother, and desirous of doing him a good turn, despatched me to him, saying "Do thou, O Sairindhri, fetch wine from Kichaka's quarters!" On beholding me the Suta's son at first addressed me in sweet words, and when that failed, he became exceedingly enraged, and intended to use violence. Understanding the purpose of the wicked Kichaka, I speedily rushed towards the place where the king was. Felling me on the ground the wretch then kicked me in the very presence of the king himself and before the eyes of Kanka and many others, including charioteers, and royal favourites, and elephant-riders, and citizens. I rebuked the king and Kanka again and again. The king, however, neither prevented Kichaka, nor inflicted any chastisement on him. The principal ally of king Virata in war, the cruel Kichaka reft of virtue is loved by both the king and the queen. O exalted one, brave, proud, sinful, adulterous, and engrossed in all objects of enjoyment, he earneth immense wealth (from the king), and robs the possessions of others even if they cry in distress. And he never walketh in the path of virtue, nor doth he any virtuous act. Of wicked soul, and vicious disposition, haughty and villainous, and always afflicted by the shafts of Kama, though repulsed repeatedly, if he sees me again, he will outrage me. I shall then surely renounce my life. Although striving to acquire virtue (on my death) your highly meritorious acts will come to naught. Ye that are now obeying your pledge, ye will lose your wife. By protecting one's wife one's offspring are protected, and by protecting one's offspring, one's own self is protected. And it is because one begets one's own self in one's wife that the wife is called *Jaya* 15 by the wise. The husband also should be protected by the wife, thinking,—*How else will he take his birth in my womb*?—I have heard it from Brahmanas expounding the duties of the several orders that a Kshatriya hath no other duty than subduing enemies. Alas, Kichaka kicked me in the very presence of Yudhishthira the Just, and also of thyself, O Bhimasena of mighty strength. It was thou, O Bhima, that didst deliver me from the terrible Jatasura. It was thou also that with thy brothers didst vanquish Jayadratha. Do thou now slay this wretch also who hath insulted me. Presuming upon his being a favourite of the king, Kichaka, O Bharata, hath enhanced my woe. Do thou, therefore, smash this lustful wight even like an earthen pot dashed upon a stone. If, O Bharata, tomorrow's sun sheds his rays upon him who is the source of many griefs of mine, I shall, surely, mixing poison (with some drink), drink it up,—for I never shall yield to Kichaka. Far better it were, O Bhima, that I should die before thee.'"

Vaisampayana continued, "Having said this, Krishna, hiding her face in Bhima's breast began to weep. And Bhima, embracing her, consoled her to the best of his power. And having abundantly consoled that slender-waisted daughter of Drupada by means of words fraught with grave reason and sense, he wiped with his hands her face flooded with tears. And thinking of Kichaka and licking with his tongue the corners of his mouth, Bhima, filled with wrath thus spake to that distressed lady."

SECTION XXII

"Bhima said, 'I will, O timid one, do even as thou sayest. I will presently slay Kichaka with all his friends. O Yajnaseni of sweet smiles, tomorrow evening, renouncing sorrow and grief, manage to have a meeting with Kichaka. The dancing-hall that the king of the Matsya hath caused to be erected is used by the girls for dancing during the day. They repair, however, to their homes at night. There in that hall, is an excellent and well-placed wooden bed-stead. Even there I will make him see the spirits of his deceased grandsires. But, O beautiful one, when thou holdest converse with him, thou must manage it so that others may not espy thee.'"

Vaisampayana continued, "Having thus conversed with others, and shed tears in grief, they waited for the dawn of that night with painful impatience. And when the night had passed away, Kichaka, rising in the morning, went to the palace, and accosted Draupadi saying, 'Throwing thee down in the court I kicked thee in the presence of the king. Attacked by mighty self, thou couldst not obtain protection. This Virata is in name only the king of the Matsyas. Commanding the forces of this realm it is I, who am the real lord of the Matsyas. Do thou, O timid one, accept me cheerfully. I shall become thy slave. And, O thou of graceful hips, I will immediately give thee a hundred *nishkas*, and engage a hundred male and a hundred female servants (to tend thee), and will also bestow on thee cars yoked with she-mules. O timid lady, let our union take place.' Draupadi replied, 'O Kichaka, know even this is my condition. Neither thy friends nor thy brothers should know thy union with me. I am a terror of detection by those illustrious Gandharvas. Promise me this, and I yield to thee.' Hearing this Kichaka said, 'I will, O thou of graceful hips, do even as thou sayest. Afflicted by the god of love, I will, O beauteous damsel, alone repair to thy abode for union with thee, O thou of thighs round and tapering like the trunks of the plantain,—so that those Gandharvas, effulgent as the sun, may not come to know of this act of thine.' Draupadi said, 'Do thou, when it is dark, go to the dancing-hall erected by the king of the Matsyas where the girls dance during the day, repairing to their respective homes at night. The Gandharvas do not know that place. We shall then without doubt, escape all censure.'"

Vaisampayana continued, "Reflecting on the subject of her conversation with Kichaka, that half a day seemed to Krishna as long as a whole month. And the stupid Kichaka also, not knowing that it was Death that had assumed the form of a *Sairindhri*, returning home experienced the greatest delight. And deprived of sense by lust, Kichaka became speedily engaged in embellishing his person with unguents and garlands and ornaments. And while he was doing all this, thinking of that damsel of large eyes, the day seemed to him to be without an end. And the beauty of Kichaka, who was about to forsake his beauty for ever, seemed to heighten, like the wick of a burning lamp about to expire. And reposing the fullest confidence in Draupadi, Kichaka, deprived of his senses by lust and absorbed in the contemplation of expected meeting, did not even perceive that the day had departed. Meanwhile, the beautiful Draupadi approaching her husband Bhima of the Kuru race, stood before him in the kitchen. And that lady with tresses ending in beautiful curls then spake unto him, saying, 'O chastiser of foes, even as thou hadst directed, I have given Kichaka to understand that our meeting will take place in the dancing-hall. Alone will he come at night to the empty hall. Slay him there, O thou of mighty arms. Do thou, O son of Kunti, repair to that dancing-hall, and take the life, O Pandava, of Kichaka, that son of a *Suta* intoxicated with vanity. From vanity alone, that son of a *Suta* slights the Gandharvas. O best of smiters, lift him up from the earth even as Krishna had lifted up the *Naga* (Kaliya) from the Yamuna. O Pandava, afflicted as I am with grief, wipe thou my tears, and blessed be thou, protect thy own honour and that of thy race.'

"Bhima said, 'Welcome, O beauteous lady. Except the glad tidings thou bringest me, I need, O thou of exceeding beauty, no other aid whatever. The delight that I feel, O thou of great beauty, on hearing from thee about my coming encounter with Kichaka, is equal to what I felt in slaying Hidimva. I swear unto thee by Truth, by my brothers, and by morality, that I will slay Kichaka even as the lord of the celestials slew Vritra. Whether secretly or openly, I will crush Kichaka, and if the Matsyas fight for him, then I will slay them too. And slaying Duryodhana afterwards, I shall win back the earth. Let Yudhishthira, the son of Kunti, continue to pay homage unto the king of Matsya.' Hearing these words of Bhima, Draupadi said, 'In order that, O lord, thou mayst not have to renounce the truth already pledged to me, do thou, O hero, slay Kichaka in secret.' Bhima assuring her said, 'Even today I shall slay Kichaka together with his friends unknown to others during the darkness of the night. I shall, O faultless lady, crush, even as an elephant crusheth a *vela* fruit, 16 the head of the wicked Kichaka who wisheth for what is unattainable by him!'"

Vaisampayana continued, "Repairing first to the place of assignation at night, Bhima sat down, disguising himself. And he waited there in expectation of Kichaka, like a lion lying in wait for a deer. And Kichaka, having embellished his person as he chose, came to the dancing-hall at the appointed time in the hope of meeting Panchali. And thinking of the assignation, he entered the chamber. And having entered that hall enveloped in deep gloom, that wretch of wicked soul came upon Bhima of incomparable prowess, who had come a little before and who was waiting in a corner. And as an insect approacheth towards a flaming fire, or a puny animal towards a lion, Kichaka approached Bhima, lying down in a bed and burning in anger at the thought of the insult offered to Krishna, as if he were the Suta's Death. And having approached Bhima, Kichaka possessed by lust, and his heart and soul filled with ecstacy smilingly said, 'O thou of pencilled eye-brows, to thee I have already given many and various kinds of wealth from the stores earned by me, as well as hundred maids and many fine robes, and also a mansion with an inner apartment adorned with beauteous and lovely and youthful maid servants and embellished by every kind of sports and amusements. And having set all those apart for thee, I have speedily come hither. And all on a sudden, women have begun to praise me, saying, *There is not in this world any other person like unto thee in beauty and dress*!' Hearing this, Bhima said, 'It is well that thou art handsome, and it is well thou praisest thyself. I think, however, that thou hadst never before this such pleasurable touch! Thou hast an acute touch, and knowest the ways of gallantry. Skilled in the art of love-making, thou art a favourite with women. There is none like thee in this world!'"

Vaisampayana continued, "Saying this, that son of Kunti, the mighty-armed Bhima of terrible prowess, suddenly rose up, and laughingly said, 'Thy sister, O wretch, shall today behold thee dragged by me to the ground, like a mighty elephant, huge as a mountain, dragged to the ground by a lion. Thyself slain *Sairindhri* will live in peace, and we, her husbands, will also live in peace.' Saying this, the mighty Bhima seized Kichaka by the hairs of his head, which were adorned with garlands. And thus seized with force by the hair, that foremost of mighty persons, Kichaka, quickly freed his hair and grasped the arms of Bhima. And then between those lions among men, fired with wrath, between that chief of the Kichaka clan, and that best of men, there ensued a hand-to-hand encounter, like that between two powerful elephants for a female elephant in the season of spring, or like that which happened in days of yore between those lions among monkeys, the brothers Vali and Sugriva. And both equally infuriate and both eager for victory, both those combatants raised their arms resembling snakes furnished with five hoods, and attacked each other with their nails and teeth, wrought up to frenzy of wrath. Impetuously assailed by the powerful Kichaka in that encounter, the resolute Bhima did not waver a single step. And locked in each other's embraces and dragging each other, they fought on like two mighty bulls. And having nails and teeth for their weapons, the encounter between them was fierce and terrible like that of two furious tigers. And felling each other in fury, they encountered each other like a couple of elephants with rent temples. And the mighty Bhima then seized Kichaka, and Kichaka, that foremost of strong persons threw Bhima down with violence. And as those mighty combatants fought on, the crash of their arms produced a loud noise that resembled the clatter of splitting bamboos. Then Vrikodara throwing Kichaka down by main force within the room, began to toss him about furiously even as a hurricane tosseth a tree. And attacked thus in battle by the powerful Bhima, Kichaka grew weak and began to tremble. For all that, however, he tugged at the Pandava to the best of his power. And attacking Bhima, and making him wave a little, the mighty Kichaka struck him with his knees and brought him down to the ground. And overthrown by the powerful Kichaka, Bhima quickly rose up like Yama himself with mace in hand. And thus that powerful *Suta* and the Pandava, intoxicated with strength and challenging each other, grappled with each other at midnight in that solitary place. And as they roared at each other in wrath, that excellent and strong edifice began to shake every moment. And slapped on the chest by the mighty Bhima, Kichaka fired with wrath moved not a single pace. And bearing for a moment only that onslaught incapable of being born on earth, the *Suta*, overpowered by Bhima's might, became enfeebled. And seeing him waning weak, Bhima endued with great strength forcibly drew Kichaka towards his breast, and began to press hard. And breathing hard again and again in wrath, that best of victors, Vrikodara, forcibly seized Kichaka by the hair. And having seized Kichaka, the mighty Bhima began to roar like a hungry tiger that hath killed a large animal. And finding him exceedingly exhausted, Vrikodara bound him fast with his arms, as one binds a beast with a cord. And then Bhima began for a long while, to whirl the senseless Kichaka, who began to roar frightfully like a broken trumpet. 17 And in order to pacify Krishna's wrath Vrikodara grasped Kichaka's throat with his arms and began to squeeze it. And assailing with his knees the waist of that worst of the Kichakas, all the limbs of whose body had been broken into fragments and whose eye-lids were closed, Vrikodara slew him, as one would slay a beast. And beholding Kichaka entirely motionless, the son of Pandu began to roll him about on the ground. And Bhima then said, 'Slaying this wretch who intended to violate our wife,—this thorn in the side of *Sairindhri*, I am freed from the debt I owed to my brothers, and have attained perfect peace.' And having said this, that foremost of men, with eyes red in wrath, relinquished his hold of

Kichaka, whose dress and ornaments had been thrown off his person, whose eyes were rolling, and whose body was yet trembling. And that foremost of mighty persons, squeezing his own hands, and biting his lips in rage, again attacked his adversary and thrust his arms and legs and neck and head into his body like the wielder of the *Pinaka* reducing into shapeless mass the deer, which form sacrifice had assumed in order to escape his ire. And having crushed all his limbs, and reduced him into a ball of flesh, the mighty Bhimasena showed him unto Krishna. And endued with mighty energy that hero then addressed Draupadi, that foremost of all women, saying, 'Come princess of Panchala, and see what hath become of that lustful wretch!' And saying this, Bhima of terrible prowess began to press with his feet the body of that wicked wight. And lighting a torch then and showing Draupadi the body of Kichaka, that hero addressed her, saying, 'O thou of tresses ending in beautiful curls, those that solicit thee, endued as thou art with an excellent disposition and every virtue, will be slain by me even as this Kichaka hath been, O timid one.' And having accomplished that difficult task so highly agreeable to Krishna—having indeed slain Kichaka and thereby pacified his wrath, Bhima bade farewell to Krishna, the daughter of Drupada, and quickly went back to the kitchen. And Draupadi also, that best of women, having caused Kichaka to be slain had her grief removed and experienced the greatest delight. And addressing the keepers of the dancing-hall, she said, 'Come ye and behold Kichaka who had violated after other people's wives lieth down here, slain by my Gandharva husbands.' And hearing these words the guards of the dancing hall soon came by thousands to that spot, torches in hand. And repairing to that room, they beheld the lifeless Kichaka thrown on the ground, drenched with blood. And beholding him without arms and legs, they were filled with grief. And as they gazed at Kichaka, they were struck with amazement. And seeing that superhuman act, viz., the overthrow of Kichaka, they said, 'Where is his neck, and where are his legs?' And beholding him in this plight they all concluded that he had been killed by a Gandharva."

SECTION XXII

Vaisampayana said, "Then all the relatives of Kichaka, arriving at that place, beheld him there and began to wail aloud, surrounding him on all sides. And beholding Kichaka with every limb mangled, and lying like a tortoise dragged to dry ground from the water, all of them were overcome with exceeding fright, and the bristles of their bodies stood on end. And seeing him crushed all over by Bhima, like a Danava by Indra, they proceeded to take him outside, for performing his funeral obsequies. And then those persons of the *Suta* clan thus assembled together espied Krishna of faultless limbs hard by, who stood reclining on a pillar. And all the Kichakas assembled there, exclaimed, 'Let this unchaste woman be slain for whom Kichaka hath himself lost his life. Or, without slaying her here, let us cremate her with him that had lusted after her,—for it behoveth us to accomplish in every way what is agreeable to that deceased son of *Suta*.' And then they addressed Virata, saying, 'It is for her sake that Kichaka hath lost his life. Let him, therefore, be cremated along with her. It behoveth thee to grant this permission.' Thus addressed by them, king Virata, O monarch, knowing fully well the prowess of the *Suta* gave his assent to *Sairindhri* being burnt along with the *Suta's* son. And at this, the Kichakas approaching the frightened and stupefied Krishna of lotus-like eyes, seized her with violence. And binding that damsel of slender waist and placing her upon the bier, they set out with great energy towards the cemetery. And, O king, while thus forcibly carried towards the cemetery by those sons of the *Suta* tribe, the blameless and chaste Krishna living under the protections of her lords, then wailed aloud for the help of her husbands, saying, 'Oh, let Jaya, and Jayanta, and Vijaya and Jayatsena, and Jayadvala listen to my words. The *Sutas* are taking me away. Let those illustrious Gandharvas endued with speed of hand, the clatter of whose cars is loud and the twang of whose bowstrings in the midst of the mighty conflict are heard like the roar of thunder, listen to my words,—the *Sutas* are taking me away!'"

Vaisampayana continued, "Hearing those sorrowful words and lamentations of Krishna, Bhima, without a moment's reflection started up from his bed and said, 'I have heard, O *Sairindhri* the words thou hast spoken. Thou hast, therefore, O timid lady, no more fear at the hands of the *Sutas*.'"

Vaisampayana continued, "Having said this, the mighty-armed Bhima desirous of slaying the Kichakas, began to swell his body. And carefully changing his attire, he went out of the palace by a wrong egress. And climbing over a wall by the aid of a tree, he proceeded towards the cemetery whither the Kichakas had gone. And having leapt over the wall, and gone out of the excellent city, Bhima impetuously rushed to where the *Sutas* were. And, O monarch, proceeding towards the funeral pyre he beheld a large tree, tall as palmyra-palm, with gigantic shoulders and withered top. And that slayer of foes grasping with his arms that tree measuring ten *Vyamas*, uprooted it, even like an elephant, and placed it upon his shoulders. And taking up that tree with trunk and branches and measuring ten *Vyamas*, that mighty hero rushed towards the *Sutas*, like Yama himself, mace in hand. And by the impetus of his rush 18 banians and peepals and *Kinsukas* falling down on the earth lay in clusters. And beholding that Gandharva approach them like a lion in fury, all the *Sutas* trembling with fear and greatly distressed, became panic-struck. And they addressed each other, saying, 'Lo, the powerful Gandharva cometh hither, filled with rage, and with an upraised tree in hand. Let *Sairindhri*, therefore, from whom this danger of ours hath arisen, be set free.' And beholding the tree that had been uprooted by Bhimasena, they set Draupadi free and ran breathlessly towards the city. And seeing them run away, Bhima, that mighty son of the Wind-god, despatched, O foremost of kings, by means of that tree, a hundred and five of them unto the abode of Yama, like the wielder of the thunderbolt slaying the Danavas. And setting Draupadi free from her bonds, he then, O king, comforted her. And that mighty-armed and irrepressible Vrikodara, the son of Pandu, then addressed the distressed princess of Panchala with face bathed in tears, saying, 'Thus, O timid one, are they slain that wrong thee without cause. Return, O Krishna, to the city. Thou hast no longer any fear; I myself will go to the Virata's kitchen by another route.'"

Vaisampayana continued, "It was thus, O Bharata, that a hundred and five of those Kichakas were slain. And their corpses lay on the ground, making the place look like a great forest overspread with uprooted trees after a hurricane. Thus fell those hundred and five Kichakas. And including Virata's general slain before, the slaughtered Sutas numbered one hundred and six. And beholding that exceedingly wonderful feat, men and women that assembled together, were filled with astonishment. And the power of speech, O Bharata, was suspended in every one."

SECTION XXIV

Vaisampayana said, "And beholding the Sutas slain, the citizens went to the king, and represented unto him what had happened, saying, 'O king, those mighty sons of the Sutas have all been slain by the Gandharvas. Indeed, they lie scattered on the earth like huge peaks of mountains riven by thunder. *Sairindhri* also, having been set free, returneth to thy palace in the city. Alas, O king, if *Sairindhri* cometh, thy entire kingdom will be endangered. *Sairindhri* is endued with great beauty; the Gandharvas also are exceedingly powerful. Men again, without doubt, are naturally sexual. Devise, therefore, O king, without delay, such means that in consequence of wrongs done to *Sairindhri,* thy kingdom may not meet with destruction.' Hearing those words of theirs, Virata, that lord of hosts, said unto them, 'Do ye perform the last rites of the Sutas. Let all the Kichakas be burnt, in one blazing pyre with gems and fragrant unguents in profusion.' And filled with fear, the king then addressed his queen Sudeshna, saying, 'When *Sairindhri* comes back, do thou tell her these words from me, "Blessed be thou, O fair-faced *Sairindhri*. Go thou whithersoever thou likest. The king hath been alarmed, O thou of graceful hips, at the defeat already experienced at the hands of the Gandharvas. Protected as thou art by the Gandharvas, I dare not personally say all this to thee. A woman, however, cannot offend, and it is for this that I tell thee all this through a woman."'"

Vaisampayana continued, "Thus delivered by Bhimasena after the slaughter of the Sutas, the intelligent and youthful Krishna relieved from all her fears, washed her limbs and clothes in water, and proceeded towards the city, like a doe frightened by a tiger. And beholding her, the citizens, O king, afflicted with the fear of the Gandharvas fled in all directions. And some of them went so far as to shut their eyes. And then, O king, at the gate of the kitchen, the princess of Panchala saw Bhimasena staying, like an infuriate elephant of gigantic proportions. And looking upon him with wonder-expanded eyes, Draupadi, by means of words intelligible to them alone, said, 'I bow unto that prince of the Gandharvas, who hath rescued me.' At these words of her, Bhima said, 'Hearing these words of hers in obedience to whom those persons were hitherto living in the city, they will henceforth range here, regarding themselves as freed from the debt.'" 19

Vaisampayana continued, "Then she beheld the mighty-armed Dhananjaya, in the dancing-hall instructing king Virata's daughters in dancing. And issuing with Arjuna from the dancing-hall, all those damsels came to Krishna who had arrived there, and who had been persecuted so sorely, all innocent though she was. And they said, 'By good luck also it is, O *Sairindhri,* that thou hast been delivered from thy dangers. By good luck it is that thou hast returned safe. And by good luck also it is that those Sutas have been slain that had wronged thee, innocent though thou art.' Hearing this, Vrihannala said, 'How hast thou, O *Sairindhri,* been delivered? And how have those sinful wretches been slain? I wish to learn all this from thee exactly as it occurred.' *Sairindhri* replied, 'O blessed Vrihannala, always passing thy days happily in the apartments of the girls, what concern hast thou with *Sairindhri's* fate to say? Thou hast no grief to bear that *Sairindhri* hath to bear! It is for this, that thou askest me thus, distressed as I am in ridicule.' Thereat Vrihannala said, 'O blessed one, Vrihannala also hath unparalleled sorrows of her own. She hath become as low as a brute. Thou dost not, O girl, understand this. I have lived with thee, and thou too hast lived with us. When, therefore, thou art afflicted with misery, who is it that will not, O thou of beautiful hips, feel it? But no one can completely read another's heart. Therefore it is, O amiable one, that thou knowest not my heart!'"

Vaisampayana continued, "Then Draupadi, accompanied by those girls entered the royal abode, desirous of appearing before Sudeshna. And when she came before the queen, Virata's wife addressed her at the command of the king, saying, 'Do thou, O *Sairindhri,* speedily go whithersoever thou likest. The king, good betide thee, hath been filled with fear at this discomfiture at the hands of the Gandharvas. Thou art, O thou of graceful eye-brows, young and unparalleled on earth in beauty. Thou art, besides, an object of desire with men. The Gandharvas again, are exceedingly wrathful.' Thereat *Sairindhri* said, 'O beauteous lady, let the king suffer me to live here for only thirteen days more. Without doubt, the Gandharvas also will be highly obliged at this. They will then convey me hence and do what would be agreeable to Virata. Without doubt, the king, by doing this, with his friends, will reap great benefit.'"

SECTION XXV

Vaisampayana said, "At the slaughter of Kichaka and brothers, people, O king, thinking of this terrible feat, were filled with surprise. And in the city and the provinces it was generally bruited about that for bravery the king's Vallava and Kichaka were both mighty warriors. The wicked Kichaka, however, had been an oppressor of men and a dishonourer of other people's wives. And it was for this that wicked of sinful soul had been slain by the Gandharvas. And it was thus, O king, that people began to speak, from province to province of the invincible Kichaka, that slayer of hostile ranks.

"Meanwhile, the spies employed by Dhritarashtra's son, having searched various villages and towns and kingdoms and done all that they had been commanded to do and completed their examination, in the manner directed, of the countries indicated in their orders, returned to Nagarupa, gratified with at least one thing that they had learnt. 20 And seeing Dhritarashtra's son king Duryodhana of the Kuru race seated in his court with Drona and Karna and Kripa, with the high-souled Bhishma, his own brothers, and those great warriors—the Trigartas, they addressed him, saying, 'O lord of men, great hath been the care always bestowed by us in the search after the sons of Pandu in that mighty forest. Searched have we through the solitary wilderness abounding with deer and other animals and overgrown with trees and creepers of diverse kind. Searched have we also in arbours of matted woods and plants and creepers of every species, but we have failed in discovering that track by which Pritha's son of irrepressible energy may have gone. Searched have we in these and other places for their foot-prints. Searched have we closely, O king, on mountain tops and in inaccessible fastnesses, in various kingdoms and provinces teeming with people, in encampments and cities. No trace have yet been found of the sons of Pandu. Good betide thee, O bull among men, it seems that they have perished without leaving a mark behind. O foremost of warriors, although we followed in the track of those warriors, yet, O best of men, we soon lost their footprints and do not know their present residence. O lord of men, for some time we followed in the wake of their charioteers. And making our inquiries duly, we truly ascertained what we desired to know. O slayer of foes, the charioteers reached Dwaravati without the sons of Pritha among them. O king, neither the sons of Pandu, nor the chaste Krishna, are in that city of Yadavas. O bull of the Bharata race, we have not been able to discover either their track or their present abode. Salutations to thee, they are gone for good. We are acquainted with the disposition of the sons of Pandu and know something of the feats achieved by them. It behoveth thee, therefore, O lord of men, to give us instructions, O monarch, as to what we should next do in the search after the sons of Pandu. O hero, listen also to these agreeable words of ours, promising great good to thee. King Matsya's commander, Kichaka of wicked soul, by whom the Trigartas, O monarch, were repeatedly vanquished and slain with mighty force, now lieth low on the ground with all his brothers, slain, O monarch, by invisible Gandharvas during the hours of darkness, O thou of unfading glory. Having heard this delightful news about the discomfiture of our enemies, we have been exceedingly gratified, O Kauravya. Do thou now ordain what should next be done.'"

SECTION XXVI

(Go-harana Parva)

Vaisampayana said, "Having listened to these words of his spies, king Duryodhana reflected inwardly for some time and then addressed his courtiers, saying, 'It is difficult to ascertain the course of events definitely. Discern ye all, therefore, whither the sons of Pandu have gone, of this thirteenth year which they are to pass undiscovered by us all, the greater part hath already expired. What remains is by much the smaller. If, indeed, the sons of Pandu can pass undiscovered what remains of this year, devoted to the vow of truth as they are, they will then have fulfilled their pledge. They will then return like mighty elephants with temporal juice trickling down, or like snakes of virulent poison. Filled with wrath, they will, without doubt, be inflicters of terrible chastisement on the Kurus. It behoveth ye, therefore, to make such efforts without loss of time as may induce the sons of Pandu, acquainted as they are with the proprieties of time, and staying as they now are in painful disguise, to re-enter the woods suppressing their rage. Indeed, adopt ye such means as may remove all causes of quarrel and anxiety from the kingdom, making it tranquil and foeless and incapable of sustaining a diminution of territory.' Hearing these words of Duryodhana, Karna said, 'Let other spies, abler and more cunning, and capable of accomplishing their object, quickly go hence, O Bharata. Let them, well-disguised, wander through swelling kingdoms and populous provinces, prying into assemblies of the learned and delightful retreats of provinces. In the inner apartments of palaces, in shrines and holy spots, in mines and diverse other regions, the sons of Pandu should be searched after with well-directed eagerness. Let the sons of Pandu who are living in disguise be searched after by well-skilled spies in large numbers, devoted to their work, themselves well-disguised, and all well-acquainted with the objects of their search. Let the search be made on the banks of rivers, in holy regions, in villages and towns, in retreats of ascetics, in delightful mountains and mountain-caves.' When Karna ceased, Duryodhana's second brother Duhsasana, wedded to a sinful disposition, then addressed his eldest brother and said, 'O monarch, O lord of men, let those spies only in whom we have confidence, receiving their rewards in advance, once more go after the search. This and what else hath been said by Karna have our fullest approval. Let all the spies engage themselves in the search according to the directions already given. Let these and others engage in the search from province to province according to approved rules. It is my belief, however, that the track the Pandavas have followed or their present abode or occupation will not be discovered. Perhaps, they are closely concealed; perhaps, they have gone to the other side of the ocean. Or, perhaps, proud as they are of their strength and courage, they have been devoured by wild beasts; or perhaps, having been overtaken by some unusual danger, they have perished for eternity. Therefore, O prince of the Kuru race, dispelling all anxieties from thy heart, achieve what thou wilt, always acting according to thy energy.'"

SECTION XXVII

Vaisampayana said, "Endued with mighty energy and possessed of great discernment, Drona then said, 'Persons like the sons of Pandu never perish nor undergo discomfiture. Brave and skilled in every science, intelligent and with senses under control, virtuous and grateful and obedient to the virtuous Yudhishthira, ever following in the wake of their eldest brother who is conversant with the conclusions of policy and virtue and profit, who is attached to them as a father, and who strictly adhereth to virtue and is firm in truth,—persons like them that are thus devoted to their illustrious and royal brother, who gifted with great intelligence, never injureth any body and who in his turn himself obeyeth his younger brothers, never perish in this way. Why, then, should not (Yudhishthira) the son of Pritha possessing a knowledge of policy, be able to restore the prosperity of his brothers who are so obedient and devoted and high-souled? It is for this that they are carefully waiting for the arrival of their opportunity. Men such as these never perish. This is what I see by my intellect. Do, therefore, quickly and without loss of time, what should now be done, after proper reflection. And let also the abode which the sons of Pandu with souls under control as regards every purpose of life, are to occupy, be now settled. Heroic and sinless and possessed of ascetic merit, the Pandavas are difficult to be discovered (within the period of non-discovery). Intelligent and possessed of every virtue, devoted to truth and versed in the principles of policy, endued with purity and holiness, and the embodiment of immeasurable energy, the son of Pritha is capable of consuming (his foes) by a glance alone of his eyes. Knowing all this, do what is proper. Let us, therefore, once more search after them, sending Brahmanas and *Charanas*, ascetics crowned with success, and others of this kind who may have a knowledge of those heroes!'"

SECTION XXVIII

Vaisampayana said, "Then that grandsire of the Bharatas, Bhishma the son of Santanu, conversant with the *Vedas*, acquainted with the proprieties of time and place, and possessing a knowledge of every duty of morality, after the conclusion of Drona's speech, applauded the words of the preceptor and spake unto the Bharatas for their benefit these words consistent with virtue, expressive of his attachment to the virtuous Yudhishthira, rarely spoken by men that are dishonest, and always meeting with the approbation of the honest. And the words that Bhishma spake were thoroughly impartial and worshipped by the wise. And the grandsire of the Kurus said, 'The words that the regenerate Drona acquainted with the truth of every affair hath uttered, are approved by me. I have no hesitation in saying so. Endued with every auspicious mark, observant of virtuous vows, possessed of Vedic lore, devoted to religious observances, conversant with various sciences, obedient to the counsels of the aged, adhering to the vow of truth, acquainted with the proprieties of time, observant of the pledge they have given (in respect of their exile), pure in their behaviour, ever adhering to the duties of the Kshatriya order, always obedient to Kesava, high-souled, possessed of great strength, and ever-bearing the burthens of the wise, those heroic ones can never wither under misfortune. Aided by their own energy, sons of Pandu who are now leading a life of concealment in obedience to virtue, will surely never perish. It is even this that my mind surmiseth. Therefore, O Bharata, I am for employing the aid of honest counsel in our behaviour towards the sons of Pandu. It would not be the policy of any wise man to cause them to be discovered now by means of spies, 21 what we should do unto the sons of Pandu, I shall say, reflecting with the aid of the intellect. Know that I shall say nothing from ill will to thee. People like me should never give such counsels to him that is dishonest, for only counsels (like those I would give) should be offered unto them that are honest. Counsels, however, that are evil, should under no circumstances be offered. He, O child, that is devoted to truth and obedient to the aged, he, indeed, that is wise, while speaking in the midst of an assembly, should under all circumstances speak the truth, if the acquisition of virtue be an object with him. I should, therefore, say that I think differently from all those people here, in respect of the abode of Yudhishthira the just in this the thirteenth year of his exile. The ruler, O child, of the city or the province where king Yudhishthira resides cannot have any misfortune. Charitable and liberal and humble and modest must the people be of the country where king Yudhishthira resides. Agreeable in speech, with passions under control, observant of truth, cheerful, healthy, pure in conduct, and skilful in work must the people be of the country where king Yudhishthira resides. The people of the place, where Yudhishthira is, cannot be envious or malicious, or vain, or proud, but must all adhere to their respective duties. Indeed, in the place where Yudhishthira resides, Vedic hymns will be chanted all around, sacrifices will be performed, the last full libations will always be poured, 22 and gifts to Brahmanas will always be in profusion. There the clouds, without doubt, pour abundant rain, and furnished with good harvest the country will ever be without fear. There the paddy will not be without grain, fruits will not be bereft of juice, floral garlands will not be without fragrance, and the conversation of men will always be full of agreeable words. There where king Yudhishthira resides, the breezes will be delicious, the meetings of men will always be friendly, and cause of fear there will be none. There kine will be plentiful, without any of them being lean-fleshed or weak, and milk and curds and butter will all be savoury and nutritious. There where king Yudhishthira resides, every kind of corn will be full of nutrition and every edible full of flavour. There where king Yudhishthira resides, the objects of all the senses, viz.,—taste, touch, smell, and hearing, will be endued with excellent attributes. There where king Yudhishthira resides, the sights and scenes will be gladdening. And the regenerate ones of that place will be virtuous and steady in observing their respective duties. Indeed, in the country where the sons of Pandu may have taken up their abode during this thirteenth year of their exile, the people will be contented and cheerful, pure in conduct and without misery of any kind. Devoted to gods and guests and the worship of these with their whole soul, they will be fond of giving away, and filled with great energy, they will all be observant of eternal virtue. There where king Yudhishthira resides, the people, eschewing all that is evil, will be desirous of achieving only what is good. Always observant of sacrifices and pure vows, and hating untruth in speech, the people of the place where king Yudhishthira may reside will always be desirous of obtaining what is good, auspicious and beneficial. There where Yudhishthira resides, the people will certainly be desirous of achieving what is good, and their hearts will always incline towards virtue, and their vows being agreeable they themselves are ever-engaged in the acquisition of religious merit. O child, that son of Pritha in whom are intelligence and charity, the highest tranquillity and undoubted forgiveness, modesty and prosperity, and fame and great energy and a love for all creatures, is incapable of being found out (now that he hath concealed himself) even by Brahmanas, let alone ordinary persons. The wise Yudhishthira is living in close disguise in regions whose characteristics I have described. Regarding his excellent mode of life, I dare not say anything more. Reflecting well upon all this, do without loss of time what thou mayst think to be beneficial, O prince of the Kuru race, if indeed, thou hast any faith in me.'"

SECTION XXIX

Vaisampayana said, "Then Saradwata's son, Kripa said, 'What the aged Bhishma hath said concerning the Pandavas is reasonable, suited to the occasion, consistent with virtue and profit, agreeable to the ear, fraught with sound reason, and worthy of him. Listen also to what I would say on this subject. It behoveth thee to ascertain the track they have followed and their abode also by means of spies, 23 and to adopt that policy which may bring about thy welfare. O child, he that is solicitous of his welfare should not disregard even an ordinary foe. What shall I say, then, O child, of the Pandavas who are thorough masters of all weapons in battle. When, therefore, the time cometh for the reappearance of the high-souled Pandavas, who, having entered the forest, 24 are now passing their days in close disguise, thou shouldst ascertain thy strength both in thy own kingdom and in those of other kings. Without doubt, the return of the Pandavas is at hand. When their promised term of exile is over, the illustrious and mighty sons of Pritha, endued with immeasurable prowess, will come hither bursting with energy. Do thou, therefore, in order to conclude an advantageous treaty with them, have recourse to sound policy and address thyself to increase thy forces and improve thy treasury. O child, ascertaining all these, reckon thou thy own strength in respect of all thy allies weak and strong. 25 Ascertaining the efficiency, and weakness, and indifference of thy forces, as also who amongst them are well-affected and who are disaffected, we should either fight the foe or make treaty with him. Having recourse to the arts of conciliation, disunion, chastisement, bribery, presents and fair behaviour, attack thy foes and subdue the weak by might, and win over thy allies and troops and by soft speeches. When thou hast (by these means) strengthened thy army and filled thy treasury, entire success will be thine. When thou hast done all this, thou wilt be able to fight with powerful enemies that may present themselves, let alone the sons of Pandu deficient in troops and animals of their own. By adopting all these expedients according to the customs of thy order, thou wilt, O foremost of men, attain enduring happiness in due time!'"

SECTION XXX

Vaisampayana said, "Discomfited before, O monarch, many a time and oft by Matsya's *Suta* Kichaka aided by the Matsyas and the Salyas, the mighty king of the Trigartas, Susarman, who owned innumerable cars, regarding the opportunity to be a favourable one, then spoke the following words without losing a moment. And, O monarch, forcibly vanquished along with his relatives by the mighty Kichaka, king Susarman, eyeing Karna in askance, spoke these words unto Duryodhana, 'My kingdom hath many a time been forcibly invaded by the king of the Matsyas. The mighty Kichaka was that king's generalissimo. Crooked and wrathful and of wicked soul, of prowess famed over all the world, sinful in deeds and highly cruel, that wretch, however, hath been slain by the Gandharvas. Kichaka being dead, king Virata, shorn of pride and his refuge gone, will, I imagine, lose all courage. I think we ought now to invade that kingdom, if it pleases thee, O sinless one, as also the illustrious Karna and all the Kauravas. The accident that hath happened is, I imagine, a favourable one for us. Let us, therefore, repair to Virata's kingdom abounding in corn. We will appropriate his gems and other wealth of diverse kinds, and let us go to share with each other as regards his villages and kingdom. Or, invading his city by force, let us carry off by thousands his excellent kine of various species. Uniting, O king, the forces of the Kauravas and the Trigartas, let us lift his cattle in droves. Or, uniting our forces well, we will check his power by forcing him to sue for peace. Or, destroying his entire host, we will bring Matsya under subjection. Having brought him under subjection by just means, we will live in our kingdom happily, while thy power also will, without doubt, be enhanced.' Hearing these words of Susarman, Karna addressed the king, saying, 'Susarman hath spoken well; the opportunity is favourable and promises to be profitable to us. Therefore, if it pleases thee, O sinless one, let us, drawing up our forces in battle array and marshalling them in divisions, speedily set out. Or, let the expedition be managed as Saradwata's son Kripa, the preceptor Drona, and the wise and aged grandsire of the Kurus may think. Consulting with each other, let us, O lord of earth, speedily set out to attain our end. What business have we with the sons of Pandu, destitute as they are of wealth, might, and prowess? They have either disappeared for good or have gone to the abode of *Yama*. We will, O king, repair without anxiety to Virata's city, and plunder his cattle and other wealth of diverse kinds.'"

Vaisampayana continued, "Accepting these words of Karna, the son of Surya, king Duryodhana speedily commanded his brother Duhsasana, born immediately after him and always obedient to his wishes, saying, 'Consulting with the elders, array without delay, our forces. We will with all the Kauravas go to the appointed place. Let also the mighty warrior, king Susarman, accompanied by a sufficient force with vehicles and animals, set out with the Trigartas for the dominions of Matsyas. And let Susarman proceed first, carefully concealing his intention. Following in their wake, we will set out the day after in close array, for the prosperous dominions of king Matsya. Let the Trigartas, however, suddenly repair to the city of Virata, and coming upon the cowherds, seize that immense wealth (of kine). We also marching in two divisions, will seize thousands of excellent kine furnished with auspicious marks.'"

Vaisampayana continued, "Then, O Lord of earth, those warriors, the Trigartas, accompanied by their infantry of terrible prowess, marched towards the south-eastern direction, intending to wage hostilities with Virata from the desire of seizing his kine. And Susarman set out on the seventh day of the dark fortnight for seizing the kine. And then, O king, on the eighth day following of the dark fortnight, the Kauravas also accompanied by all their troops, began to seize the kine by thousands."

SECTION XXXI

Vaisampayana said, "O mighty king, entering into king Virata's service, and dwelling in disguise in his excellent city, the high-souled Pandavas of immeasurable prowess, completed the promised period of non-discovery. And after Kichaka had been slain, that slayer of hostile heroes, the mighty king Virata began to rest his hopes on the sons of Kunti. And it was on the expiry of the thirteenth year of their exile, O Bharata, that Susarman seized Virata's cattle by thousands. And when the cattle had been seized, the herdsman of Virata came with great speed to the city, and saw his sovereign, the king of Matsyas, seated on the throne in the midst of wise councillors, and those bulls among men, the sons of Pandu, and surrounded by brave warriors decked with ear-rings and bracelets. And appearing before that enhancer of his dominion—King Virata seated in court—the herdsman bowed down unto him, and addressed him, saying, 'O foremost of kings, defeating and humiliating us in battle along with our friends the Trigartas are seizing thy cattle by hundreds and by thousands. Do thou, therefore, speedily rescue them. Oh, see that they are not lost to thee.' Hearing these words, the king arrayed for battle the Matsya force abounding in cars and elephants and horses and infantry and standards. And kings and princes speedily put on, each in its proper place,[26] their shining and beautiful armour worthy of being worn by heroes. And Virata's beloved brother, Satanika, put on a coat of mail made of adamantine steel, adorned with burnished gold. And Madiraksha, next in birth to Satanika, put on a strong coat of mail plated with gold[27] and capable of resisting every weapon. And the coat of mail that the king himself of the Matsyas put on was invulnerable and decked with a hundred suns, a hundred circles, a hundred spots, and a hundred eyes. And the coat of mail that Suryadatta[28] put on was bright as the sun, plated with gold, and broad as a hundred lotuses of the fragrant (*Kahlara*) species. And the coat of mail that Virata's eldest son, the heroic Sanksha, put on was impenetrable and made of burnished steel, and decked with a hundred eyes of gold. And it was thus that those god-like and mighty warriors by hundreds, furnished with weapons, and eager for battle, each donned his corselet. And then they yoked unto their excellent cars of white-hue steeds equipped in mail. And then was hoisted—Matsya's glorious standard on his excellent car decked with gold and resembling the sun or the moon in its effulgence. And other Kshatriya warriors also raised on their respective cars gold-decked standards of various shapes and devices. And king Matsya then addressed his brother Satanika born immediately after him, saying, 'Kanka and Vallava and Tantripala and Damagranthi of great energy will, as it appears to me fight, without doubt. Give thou unto them cars furnished with banners and let them case their persons in beautiful coats of mail that should be both invulnerable and easy to wear. And let them also have weapons. Bearing such martial forms and possessed of arms resembling the trunk of mighty elephants, I can never persuade myself that they cannot fight.' Hearing these words of the king, Satanika, O monarch, immediately ordered cars for those sons of Pritha, viz., the royal Yudhishthira, and Bhima, and Nakula, and Sahadeva, and commanded by the king, the charioteers, with cheerful hearts and keeping loyalty in view, very soon got cars ready (for the Pandavas). And those repressers of foes then donned those beautiful coats of mail, invulnerable and easy to wear, that Virata had ordered for those heroes of spotless fame. And mounted on cars yoked with good steeds, those smiters of hostile ranks, those foremost of men, the sons of Pritha, set out with cheerful hearts. Indeed, those mighty warriors skilled in fight, those bulls of the Kuru race and sons of Pandu, those four heroic brothers possessed of prowess incapable of being baffled, mounting on cars decked with gold, together set out, following Virata's wake. And infuriate elephants of terrible mien, full sixty years of age, with shapely tusks and rent temples and juice trickling down and looking (on that account) like cloud pouring rain and mounted by trained warriors skilled in fight, followed the king like unto moving hills. And the principal warriors of Matsya who cheerfully followed the king had eight thousand cars, a thousand elephants and sixty thousand horses. And, O bull among the Bharatas, that force of Virata, O king, as it marched forth marking the footprints of the cattle looked exceedingly beautiful. And on its march that foremost of armies owned by Virata, crowded with soldiers armed with strong weapons, and abounding in elephants, horses and cars, looked really splendid."

SECTION XXXII

Vaisampayana said, "Marching out of the city, those heroic smiters the Matsyas, arrayed in order of battle, overtook the Trigartas when the sun had passed the meridian. And both excited to fury and both desirous of having the king, the mighty Trigartas and the Matsyas, irrepressible in battle, sent up loud roars. And then the terrible and infuriate elephants ridden over by the skilful combatants of both sides were urged on with spiked clubs and hooks. And the encounter, O king, that took place when the sun was low in the horizon, between the infantry and cavalry and chariots and elephants of both parties, was like unto that of old between the gods and the *Asuras*, terrible and fierce and sufficient for making one's hair stand on end and calculated to increase the population of Yama's kingdom. And as the combatants rushed against one another, smiting and slashing, thick clouds of dust began to rise, so that nothing could be discovered. And covered with the dust raised by the contending armies, birds began to drop down on the earth. And the sun himself disappeared behind the thick cloud of arrows shot, and the firmament looked bright as if with myriads of the fireflies. And shifting their bows, the staves of which were decked with gold, from one hand to another, those heroes began to strike each other down, discharging their arrows right and left. And cars encountered cars, and foot-soldiers fought with foot-soldiers, and horse-men with horsemen, and elephants with mighty elephants. And they furiously encountered one another with swords and axes, bearded darts and javelins, and iron clubs. And although, O king, those mighty-armed warriors furiously assailed one another in that conflict, yet neither party succeeded in prevailing over the other. And severed heads, some with beautiful noses, some with upper lips deeply gashed, some decked with ear-rings, and some divided with wounds about the well-trimmed hair were seen rolling on the ground covered with dust. And soon the field of battle was overspread with the limbs of Kshatriya warriors, cut off by means of arrows and lying like trunks of *Sala* trees. And scattered over with heads decked in ear-rings, and sandal-besmeared arms looking like the bodies of snakes, the field of battle became exceedingly beautiful. And as cars encountered cars, and horsemen encountered horsemen, and foot-soldiers fought with foot-soldiers, and elephants met with elephants, the frightful dust soon became drenched with torrents of blood. And some amongst the combatants began to swoon away, and the warriors began to fight reckless of consideration of humanity, friendship and relationship. And both their course and sight obstructed by the arrowy shower, vultures began to alight on the ground. But although those strong-armed combatants furiously fought with one another, yet the heroes of neither party succeeded in routing their antagonists. And Satanika having slain a full hundred of the enemy and Visalaksha full four hundred, both those mighty warriors penetrated into the heart of the great Trigarta host. And having entered into the thick of the Trigarta host, those famous and mighty heroes began to deprive their antagonists of their senses by causing a closer conflict to set in—a conflict, in which the combatants seized one another by the hair and tore one another with their nails. 29 And eyeing the point where the cars of the Trigartas had been mustered in strong numbers, those heroes at last directed their attack towards it. And that foremost of car-warriors, king Virata also, with Suryadatta in his van and Madiraksha in his rear, having destroyed in that conflict five hundred cars, eight hundred horses, and five warriors on great cars, displayed various skilful manoeuvres on his car on that field of battle. And at last the king came upon the ruler of the Trigartas mounted on a golden chariot. And those high-souled and powerful warriors, desirous of fighting, rushed roaring against each like two bulls in a cow-pen. Then that bull among men, irrepressible in battle, Susarman, the king of the Trigartas, challenged Matsya to a single combat on car. Then those warriors excited to fury rushed against each other on their cars and began to shower their arrows upon each other like clouds pouring torrents of rain. 30 And enraged with each other, those fierce warriors, both skilled in weapons, both wielding swords and darts and maces, then moved about (on the field of battle) assailing each other with whetted arrows. Then king Virata pierced Susarman with ten shafts and each of his four horses also with five shafts. And Susarman also, irresistible in battle and conversant with fatal weapons, pierced king of Matsya with fifty whetted shafts. And then, O mighty monarch, in consequence of the dust on the field of battle, the soldiers of both Susarman and Matsya's king could not distinguish one another."

SECTION XXXIII

Vaisampayana said, "Then, O Bharata, when the world was enveloped in dust and the gloom of night, the warriors of both sides, without breaking the order of battle, desisted for a while. 31 And then, dispelling the darkness the moon arose illumining the night and gladdening the hearts of the Kshatriya warriors. And when everything became visible, the battle once more began. And it raged on so furiously that the combatants could not distinguish one another. And then Trigarta's lord, Susarman with his younger brother, and accompanied by all his cars, rushed towards the king of Matsya. And descending from their cars, those bulls among Kshatriyas, the (royal) brothers, mace in hand, rushed furiously towards the cars of the foe. And the hostile hosts fiercely assailed each other with maces and swords and scimitars, battle-axes and bearded darts with keen edges and points of excellent temper. And king Susarman, the lord of the Trigartas having by his energy oppressed and defeated the whole army of the Matsyas, impetuously rushed towards Virata himself endued with great energy. And the two brothers having severally slain Virata's two steeds and his charioteer, as also those soldiers that protected his rear, took him captive alive, when deprived of his car. Then afflicting him sorely, like a lustful man afflicting a defenceless damsel, Susarman placed Virata on his own car, and speedily rushed out of the field. And when the powerful Virata, deprived of his car, was taken captive, the Matsyas, harrassed solely by the Trigartas, began to flee in fear in all directions. And beholding them panic-stricken, Kunti's son, Yudhishthira, addressed that subduer of foes, the mighty-armed Bhima, saying, 'The king of the Matsyas hath been taken by the Trigartas. Do thou, O mighty-armed one, rescue him, so that he may not fall under the power of the enemy. As we have lived happily in Virata's city, having every desire of ours gratified, it behoveth thee, O Bhimasena, to discharge that debt (by liberating the king).' Thereat Bhimasena replied, 'I will liberate him, O king, at thy command. Mark the feat I achieve (today) in battling with the foe, relying solely on the might of my arms. Do thou, O king, stay aside, along with our brothers and witness my prowess today. Uprooting this mighty tree of huge trunk looking like a mace, I will rout the enemy.'"

Vaisampayana continued, "Beholding Bhima casting his eyes on that tree like a mad elephant, the heroic king Yudhishthira the just spake unto his brother, saying, 'Do not, O Bhima, commit such a rash act. Let the tree stand there. Thou must not achieve such feats in a super-human manner by means of that tree, for if thou dost, the people, O Bharata, will recognise thee and say, *This is Bhima*. Take thou, therefore, some human weapon such as a bow (and arrows), or a dart, or a sword, or a battle-axe. And taking therefore, O Bhima, some weapon that is human, liberate thou the king without giving anybody the means of knowing thee truly. The twins endued with great strength will defend thy wheels. Fighting together, O child, liberate the king of the Matsyas!'"

Vaisampayana continued, "Thus addressed, the mighty Bhimasena endued with great speed, quickly took up an excellent bow and impetuously shot from it a shower of arrows, thick as the downpour of a rain-charged cloud. And Bhima then rushed furiously towards Susarman of terrible deeds, and assuring Virata with the words—*O good king!* 32 said unto the lord of the Trigartas,—*Stay! Stay!* Seeing Bhima like unto Yama himself in his rear, saying, *Stay! Stay! Do thou witness this mighty feat,—this combat that is at hand!*—the bull among warriors, Susarman, seriously considered (the situation), and taking up his bow turned back, along with his brothers. Within the twinkling of an eye, Bhima destroyed those cars that sought to oppose him. And soon again hundreds of thousands of cars and elephants and horses and horsemen and brave and fierce bowmen were overthrown by Bhima in the very sight of Virata. And the hostile infantry also began to be slaughtered by the illustrious Bhima, mace in hand. And beholding that terrible onslaught, Susarman, irrepressible in fight, thought within himself, 'My brother seems to have already succumbed in the midst of his mighty host. Is my army going to be annihilated?' And drawing his bow-string to his ear Susarman then turned back and began to shoot keen-edged shafts incessantly. And seeing the Pandavas return to the charge on their car, the Matsya warriors of mighty host, urging on their steeds, shot excellent weapons for grinding the Trigarta soldiers. And Virata's son also, exceedingly exasperated began to perform prodigious fears of valour. And Kunti's son Yudhishthira slew a thousand (of the foe), and Bhima showed the abode of Yama unto seven thousand. And Nakula sent seven hundred (to their last account) by means of his shafts. And powerful Sahadeva also, commanded by Yudhishthira, slew three hundred brave warriors. And having slain such numbers, that fierce and mighty warrior, Yudhishthira, with weapons upraised, rushed against Susarman. And rushing impetuously at Susarman, that foremost of car-warriors, king Yudhishthira, assailed him with vollies of shafts. And Susarman also, in great rage, quickly pierced Yudhishthira with nine arrows, and each of his four steeds with four arrows. Then, O king, Kunti's son Bhima of quick movements, approaching Susarman crushed his steeds. And having slain also those soldiers that protected his rear, he dragged from the car his antagonist's charioteer to the ground. And seeing the king of Trigarta's car without a driver, the defender of his car-wheels, the famous and brave Madiraksha speedily came to his aid. And thereat, leaping down from Susarman's car, and securing the latter's mace the powerful Virata ran in pursuit of him. And though old, he moved on the field, mace in hand, even like a lusty youth. And beholding Susarman flee Bhima addressed him, saying, 'Desist, O Prince! This flight of thine is not proper! With this prowess of thine, how couldst thou wish to carry off the cattle by force? How also, forsaking thy follower, dost thou droop so amidst foes?' Thus addressed by Pritha's son, the mighty Susarman, that lord of countless cars saying unto Bhima, *Stay! Stay!*—suddenly turned round and rushed at him. Then Bhima, the son of Pandu, leaping down from his car, as he alone could do, 33 rushed forward with great coolness, desirous of taking Susarman's life. And desirous of seizing Trigarta's king advancing towards him, the mighty Bhimasena rushed impetuously towards him, even like a lion rushing at a small deer. And advancing impetuously, the mighty-armed Bhima seized Susarman by the hair, and lifting him up in wrath, dashed him down on the ground. And as he lay crying in agony, the mighty-armed Bhima kicked him at the head, and placing his knee on his breast dealt him severe blows. And sorely afflicted with that kicking, the king of Trigartas became senseless. And when the king of the Trigartas deprived of his car, had been seized thus, the whole Trigarta army stricken with panic, broke and fled in all directions, and the mighty sons of Pandu, endued with modesty and observant of vows and relying on the might of their own arms, after having vanquished Susarman, and rescued the kine as well as other kinds of wealth and having thus dispelled Virata's anxiety, stood together before that monarch. And Bhimasena then said, 'This wretch given to wicked deeds doth not deserve to escape me with life. But what can I do? The king is so lenient!' And then taking Susarman by the neck as he was lying on the ground insensible and covered with dust, and binding him fast, Pritha's son Vrikodara placed him on his car, and went to where Yudhishthira was staying in the midst of the field. And Bhima then showed Susarman unto the monarch. And beholding Susarman in that plight, that tiger among men king Yudhishthira smilingly addressed Bhima—that ornament of battle,—saying, 'Let this worst of men be set free.' Thus addressed, Bhima spoke unto the mighty Susarman, saying, 'If, O wretch, thou wishest to live, listen to those words of mine. Thou must say in every court and assembly of men,—*I am a slave.* On this condition only I will grant thee thy life. Verily, this is the law about the vanquished.' Thereupon his elder brother affectionately addressed Bhima, saying, 'If thou regardest us as an authority, liberate this wicked wight. He hath already become king Virata's slave.' And turning then to Susarman, he said, 'Thou art freed. Go thou a free man, and never act again in this way.'"

SECTION XXXIV

Vaisampayana said, "Thus addressed by Yudhishthira Susarman was overwhelmed with shame and hung down his head. And liberated (from slavery), he went to king Virata, and having saluted the monarch, took his departure. And the Pandavas also relying on the might of their own arms, and endued with modesty and observant of vows, having slain their enemies and liberated Susarman, passed that night happily on the field of battle. And Virata gratified those mighty warriors, the sons of Kunti, possessed of super-human prowess with wealth and honour. And Virata said, 'All these gems of mine are now as much mine as yours. Do ye according to your pleasure live here happily. And ye smiter of foes in battle, I will bestow on you damsels decked with ornaments, wealth in plenty, and other things that ye may like. Delivered from perils today by your prowess, I am now crowned with victory. Do ye all become the lords of the Matsyas.'"

Vaisampayana continued, "And when the king of the Matsyas had addressed them thus, those descendants of the Kurus with Yudhishthira at their head, joining their hands, severally replied unto him saying, 'We are well-pleased with all that thou sayest, O monarch. We, however, have been much gratified that thou hast today been freed from thy foes.' Thus answered, that foremost of kings, Virata the lord of the Matsyas, again addressed Yudhishthira, saying, 'Come, we will install thee in sovereignty of the Matsyas. And we will also bestow on thee things that are rare on earth and are objects of desire, for thou deservest everything at our hands. O foremost of Brahmanas of the *Vaiyaghra* order I will bestow on thee gems and kine and gold and rubies and pearls. I bow unto thee. It is owing to thee that I once more behold today my sons and kingdom. Afflicted and threatened as I had been with disaster and danger, it is through thy prowess that I have not succumbed to the foe.' Then Yudhishthira again addressed the Matsyas, saying, 'Well-pleased are we with the delightful words that thou hast spoken. Mayst thou be ever happy, always practising humanity towards all creatures. Let messengers now, at thy command, speedily repair into the city, in order to communicate the glad tidings to our friends, and proclaim thy victory.' Hearing these words of him, king Matsya ordered the messengers, saying, 'Do ye repair to the city and proclaim my victory in battle. And let damsels and courtesans, decked in ornaments, come out of the city with every kind of musical instruments.' Hearing this command uttered by the king of the Matsyas, the men, laying the mandate on their head, all departed with cheerful hearts. And having repaired to the city that very night, they proclaimed at the hour of sunrise the victory of the king about the city-gates."

SECTION XXXV

Vaisampayana said, "When the king of the Matsyas, anxious of recovering the kine, had set out in pursuit of the Trigartas, Duryodhana with his counsellors invaded the dominions of Virata. And Bhishma and Drona, and Karna, and Kripa acquainted with the best of weapons, Aswatthaman, and Suvala's son, and Duhsasana, O lord of men, and Vivingsati and Vikarna and Chitrasena endued with great energy, and Durmukha and Dussaha,—these and many other great warriors, coming upon the Matsya dominion speedily drove off the cowherds of king Virata and forcibly took away the kine. And the Kauravas, surrounding all sides with a multitude of cars, seized sixty thousands of kine. And loud was the yell of woe set up by the cowherds smitten by those warriors in that terrible conflict. And the chief of the cowherds, greatly affrighted speedily mounted on a chariot and set out for the city, bewailing in affliction. And entering the city of the king, he proceeded to the place, and speedily alighting from the chariot, got in for relating (what had happened). And beholding the proud son of Matsya, named Bhuminjaya, he told him everything about the seizure of the royal kine. And he said, 'the Kauravas are taking away sixty thousand kine. Rise, therefore, O enhancer of the kingdom's glory, for bringing back thy cattle. O prince, if thou art desirous of achieving (the kingdom's) good set out thyself without loss of time. Indeed, the king of the Matsyas left thee in the empty city. The king (thy father) boasteth of thee in court, saying, "My son, equal unto me, is a hero and is the supporter of (the glory of) my race. My son is a warrior skilled in arrows and weapons and is always possessed of great courage."—Oh, let the words of that lord of men be true! O chief of herd-owners, bring thou back the kine after vanquishing the Kurus, and consume thou their troops with the terrific energy of thy arrows. Do thou like a leader of elephants rushing at a herd, pierce the ranks of the foe with straight arrows of golden wings, discharged from thy bow. Thy bow is even like a *Vina*. Its two ends represent the ivory pillows; its string, the main chord; its staff, the finger-board; and the arrows shot from it musical notes. Do thou strike in the midst of the foe that *Vina* of musical sound. 34 Let thy steeds, O lord, of silvery hue, be yoked unto thy car, and let thy standard be hoisted, bearing the emblem of the golden lion. Let thy keen-edged arrows endued with wings of gold, shot by thy strong arms, obstruct the path of those kings and eclipse the very sun. Vanquishing all the Kurus in battle like unto the wielder of the thunderbolt defeating the *Asuras*, return thou again to the city having achieved great renown. Son of Matsya's king, thou art the sole refuge of this kingdom, as that foremost of virtuous warriors, Arjuna is of the sons of Pandu. Even like Arjuna of his brothers, thou art, without doubt, the refuge of those dwelling within these dominions. Indeed, we, the subject of this realm, have our protector in thee.'"

Vaisampayana continued, "Thus addressed by the cowherd in the presence of the females, in words breathing courage, the prince indulging in self-commendation within the female apartments, spoke these words."

SECTION XXXVI

"Uttara said, 'Firm as I am in the use of the bow, I would set out this very day in the track of the kine if only some one skilled in the management of horses becomes my charioteer. I do not, however, know the man who may be my charioteer. Look ye, therefore, without delay, for a charioteer for me that am prepared for starting. My own charioteer was slain in the great battle that was fought from day to day for a whole month or at least for eight and twenty nights. As soon as I get another person conversant with the management of the steeds, I will immediately set out, hoisting high my own standard. Penetrating into the midst of the hostile army abounding with elephants and horses and chariots, I will bring back the kine, having vanquished the Kurus who are feeble in strength and weak in weapons. Like a second wielder of the thunderbolt terrifying the Danavas, I will bring back the kine this very moment, affrighting in battle Duryodhana and Bhishma and Karna and Kripa and Drona with his son, and other mighty bowmen assembled for fight. Finding none (to oppose), the Kurus are taking away the kine. What can I do when I am not there? The assembled Kurus shall witness my prowess today. And they shall say unto one another, "Is it Arjuna himself who is opposing us?"'

Vaisampayana continued, "Having heard these words spoken by the prince, Arjuna fully acquainted with the import of everything, after a little while cheerfully spake in private unto his dear wife of faultless beauty, Krishna, the princess of Panchala, Drupada's daughter of slender make, sprung from the (sacrificial) fire and endued with the virtues of truthfulness and honesty and ever attentive to the good of her husbands. And the hero said, 'Do thou, O beauteous one, at my request say unto Uttara without delay, "This Vrihannala was formerly the accomplished resolute charioteer of Pandu's son (Arjuna). Tried in many a great battle, even he will be thy charioteer."'"

Vaisampayana continued, "Hearing these words uttered by the prince over and over again in the midst of the women, Panchali could not quietly bear those allusions to Vibhatsu. And bashfully stepping out from among the women, the poor princess of Panchala gently spake unto him these words, 'The handsome youth, looking like a mighty elephant and known by the name of Vrihannala, was formerly the charioteer of Arjuna. A disciple of that illustrious warrior, and inferior to none in use of the bow, he was known to me while I was living with the Pandavas. It was by him that the reins were held of Arjuna's excellent steeds when Agni consumed the forest of Khandava. It was with him as charioteer that Partha conquered all creatures at Khandava-prastha. In fact, there is no charioteer equal unto him.'

"Uttara said, 'Thou knowest, O *Sairindhri*, this youth. Thou knowest, what this one of the neuter sex may or may not be. I cannot, however, O blessed one, myself request Vrihannala to hold the reins of my horses.'

"Draupadi said, 'Vrihannala, O hero, will without doubt, obey the words of thy younger sister[35] —that damsel of graceful hips. If he consents to be thy charioteer, thou wilt, without doubt, return, having vanquished the Kurus and rescued thy kine.'

"Thus addressed by the *Sairindhri*, Uttara spake unto his sister, 'Go thyself, O thou of faultless beauty, and bring Vrihannala hither.' And despatched by her brother, she hastily repaired to the dancing-hall where that strong-armed son of Pandu was staying in disguise."

SECTION XXXVII

Vaisampayana said, "Thus despatched by her elder brother, the far-famed daughter of king Matsya, adorned with a golden necklace, ever obedient to her brother and possessed of a waist slender as that of the wasp, 36 endued with the splendour of Lakshmi herself, 37 decked with the plumes of the peacock of slender make and graceful limbs, her hips encircled by a zone of pearls, her eye-lashes slightly curved, and her form endued with every grace, hastily repaired to the dancing-hall like a flash of lightning rushing towards a mass of dark clouds. 38 And the faultless and auspicious daughter of Virata, of fine teeth and slender-waist, of thighs close unto each other and each like the trunk of an elephant, her person embellished with an excellent garland, sought the son of Pritha like a she-elephant seeking her mate. And like unto a precious gem or the very embodiment of prosperity of Indra, of exceeding beauty and large eyes, that charming and adored and celebrated damsel saluted Arjuna. And saluted by her, Partha asked that maiden of close thighs and golden complexion, saying 'What brings thee hither, a damsel decked in a necklace of gold? Why art thou in such a hurry, O gazelle-eyed maiden? Why is thy face, O beauteous lady, so cheerless? Tell me all this without delay!'"

Vaisampayana continued, "Beholding, O king, his friend, the princess of large-eyes (in that plight), her friend (Arjuna) cheerfully enquired of her (in these words) the cause of her arrival there and then. And having approached that bull among men, the princess, standing in the midst of her female attendants, the displaying proper modesty 39 , addressed him, saying, 'The kine of this realm, O Vrihannala, are being driven away by the Kurus, and it is to conquer them that my brother will set out bow in hand. Not long ago his own charioteer was slain in battle, and there is none equal unto the one slain that can act as my brother's charioteer. And unto him striving to obtain a charioteer, *Sairindhri*, O Vrihannala, hath spoken about thy skill in the management of steeds. Thou wert formerly the favourite charioteer of Arjuna, and it was with thee that that bull among the sons of Pandu had alone subjugated the whole earth. Do thou, therefore, O Vrihannala, act as the charioteer of my brother. (By this time) our kine have surely been driven away by the Kurus to a great distance. Requested by me if thou dost not act up to my words, I who am asking this service of thee out of affection, will give up my life!' Thus addressed by this friend of graceful hips, that oppressor of foes, endued with immeasurable prowess, went into the prince's presence. And like unto a she-elephant running after her young one, the princess possessed of large eyes followed that hero advancing with hasty steps like unto an elephant with rent temples. And beholding him from a distance, the prince himself said, 'With thee as his charioteer, Dhananjaya the son of Kunti had gratified *Agni* at the Khandava forest and subjugated the whole world! The *Sairindhri* hath spoken of thee to me. She knoweth the Pandavas. Do thou, therefore, O Vrihannala, hold, as thou didst, the reins of my steeds, desirous as I am of righting with the Kurus and rescuing my bovine wealth. Thou wert formerly the beloved charioteer of Arjuna and it was with thee that that bull among the sons of Pandu had alone subjugated the whole earth!' Thus addressed, Vrihannala replied unto the prince, saying, 'What ability have I to act as a charioteer in the field of battle? If it is song or dance or musical instruments or such other things, I can entertain thee therewith, but where is my skill for becoming a charioteer?'

"Uttara said, 'O Vrihannala, be thou a singer or a dancer, hold thou (for the present), without loss of time, the reins of my excellent steeds, mounting upon my car!'"

Vaisampayana continued, "Although that oppressor of foes, the son of Pandu, was acquainted with everything, yet in the presence of Uttara, he began to make many mistakes for the sake of fun. And when he sought to put the coat of mail on his body by raising it upwards, the large-eyed maidens, beholding it, burst out into a loud laughter. And seeing him quite ignorant of putting on armour, Uttara himself equipped Vrihannala with a costly coat of mail. And casing his own person in an excellent armour of solar effulgence, and hoisting his standard bearing the figure of a lion, the prince caused Vrihannala to become his charioteer. And with Vrihannala to hold his reins, the hero set out, taking with him many costly bows and a large number of beautiful arrows. And his friend, Uttara and her maidens then said unto Vrihannala, 'Do thou, O Vrihannala, bring for our dolls (when thou comest back) various kinds of good and fine cloths after vanquishing the Kurus assembled for battle of whom Bhishma and Drona are foremost!' Thus addressed, Partha the son of Pandu, in a voice deep as the roar of the clouds, smilingly said unto that bevy of fair maidens. 'If thus Uttara can vanquish those mighty warriors in battle, I will certainly bring excellent and beautiful cloths.'"

Vaisampayana continued, "Having said these words, the heroic Arjuna urged the steeds towards the Kuru army over which floated innumerable flags. Just, however, as they were starting, elderly dames and maidens, and Brahmanas of rigid vows, beholding Uttara seated on his excellent car with Vrihannala as charioteer and under that great banner hoisted on high, walked round the car to bless the hero. And the women said, 'Let the victory that Arjuna treading like a bull had achieved of old on the occasion of burning the forest of Khandava, be thine, O Vrihannala, when thou encounterest the Kurus today with prince Uttara.'"

SECTION XXXVIII

Vaisampayana said, "Having issued forth from the city, the dauntless son of Virata addressed his charioteer, saying, 'Proceed whither the Kurus are. Defeating the assembled Kurus who have come hither from desire of victory, and quickly rescuing my kine from them, I will return to the capital.' At these words of the prince, the son of Pandu urged those excellent steeds. And endued with the speed of the wind and decked with necklaces of gold, those steeds, urged by that lion among men, seemed to fly through the air. And they had not proceeded far when those smiters of foes, Dhananjaya and the son of Matsya, sighted the army of the powerful Kurus. And proceeding towards the cemetery, they came upon the Kurus and beheld their army arrayed in order of battle. 40 And that large army of theirs looked like the vast sea or a forest of innumerable trees moving through the sky. And then was seen, O best among the Kurus, the dust raised by that moving army which reached the sky and obstructed the sight of all creatures. And beholding that mighty host abounding in elephants, horses and chariots, and protected by Karna and Duryodhana and Kripa and Santanu's son, and that intelligent and great bowman Drona, with his son (Aswatthaman), the son of Virata, agitated with fear and the bristles on his body standing on their ends, thus spake unto Partha, 'I dare not fight with the Kurus. See, the bristles on my body have stood on their ends. I am incapable of battling with this countless host of the Kurus, abounding in the heroic warriors, that are extremely fierce and difficult of being vanquished even by the celestials. I do not venture to penetrate into the army of the Bharatas consisting of terrible bowmen and abounding in horses and elephants and cars and footsoldiers and banners. My mind is too much perturbed by the very sight of the foe on the field of battle on which stand Drona and Bhishma, and Kripa, and Karna, and Vivingsati, and Aswatthaman and Vikarna, and Saumadatti, and Vahlika, and the heroic king Duryodhana also—that foremost of car-warriors, and many other splendid bowmen, all skilled in battle. My hairs have stood on their ends, and I am fainting with fear at the very sight of these smiters, the Kurus arrayed in order of battle.'"

Vaisampayana continued, "And the low-minded and foolish Uttara out of folly alone, began to bewail (his fate) in the presence of the high-spirited (Arjuna) disguised (as his charioteer) in these words, 'My father hath gone out to meet the Trigartas taking with him his whole army, leaving me in the empty city. There are no troops to assist me. Alone and a mere boy who has not undergone much exercise in arms, I am unable to encounter these innumerable warriors and all skilled in weapons. Do thou, therefore, O Vrihannala, cease to advance!'

"Vrihannala said, 'Why dost thou look so pale through fear and enhance the joy of thy foes? As yet thou hast done nothing on the field of battle with the enemy. It was thou that hadst ordered me, saying, *Take me towards the Kauravas*. I will, therefore, take thee, thither where those innumerable flags are. I will certainly take thee, O mighty-armed one, into the midst of the hostile Kurus, prepared to fight as they are for the kine like hawks for meat. I would do this, even if I regarded them to have come hither for battling for a much higher stake such as the sovereignty of the earth. Having, at the time of setting out, talked before both men and women so highly of thy manliness, why wouldst thou desist from the fight? If thou shouldst return home without recapturing the kine, brave men and even women, when they meet together, will laugh at thee (in derision). As regards myself, I cannot return to the city without having rescued the kine, applauded as I have been so highly by the *Sairindhri* in respect of my skill in driving cars. It is for those praises by the *Sairindhri* and for those words of thine also (that I have come). Why should I not, therefore, give battle to the Kurus? (As regards thyself), be thou still.'

"Uttara said, 'Let the Kurus rob the Matsyas of all their wealth. Let men and women, O Vrihannala, laugh at me. Let my kine perish, let the city be a desert. Let me stand exposed before my father. Still there is no need of battle.'"

Vaisampayana continued, "Saying this, that much affrighted prince decked in ear-ring jumped down from his car, and throwing down his bow and arrows began to flee, sacrificing honour and pride. Vrihannala, however, exclaimed, 'This is not the practice of the brave, this flight of a Kshatriya from the field of battle. Even death in battle is better than flight from fear.' Having said this, Dhananjaya, the son of Kunti, coming down from that excellent car ran after that prince thus running away, his own long braid and pure red garments fluttering in the air. And some soldiers, not knowing that it was Arjuna who was thus running with his braid fluttering in the air, burst out into laughter at the sight. And beholding him thus running, the Kurus began to argue, 'Who is this person, thus disguised like fire concealed in ashes? He is partly a man and partly a woman. Although bearing a neuter form, he yet resembleth Arjuna. His are the same head and neck, and his the same arms like unto a couple of maces. And this one's gait also is like unto his. He can be none else than Dhananjaya. As *Indra* is among the celestials, so Dhananjaya is among men. Who else in this world than Dhananjaya, would alone come against us? Virata left a single son of his in the empty city. He hath come out from childishness and not from true heroism. It is Uttara who must have come out of the city, having, without doubt, made as a charioteer Arjuna, the son of Pritha, now living in disguise. It seems that he is now flying away in panic at sight of our army. And without doubt Dhananjaya runneth after him to bring him back.'"

Vaisampayana continued, "Beholding the disguised son of Pandu, the Kauravas, O Bharata, began to indulge in these surmises, but they could not come to any definite conclusion. Meanwhile, Dhananjaya, hastily pursuing the retreating Uttara, seized him by the hair within a hundred steps. And seized by Arjuna, the son of Virata began to lament most woefully like one in great affliction, and said, 'Listen, O good Vrihannala, O thou of handsome waist. Turn thou quickly the course of the car. He that liveth meeteth with prosperity. I will give thee a hundred coins of pure gold and eight *lapis lazuli* of great brightness set with gold, and one chariot furnished with a golden flag-staff and drawn by excellent steeds, and also ten elephants of infuriate prowess. Do thou, O Vrihannala, set me free.'"

Vaisampayana continued, "Thus addressed, that tiger among men laughingly dragged Uttara who was almost deprived of his senses and who was uttering these words of lamentation towards the car. And the son of Pritha then addressed the affrighted prince who had nearly lost his senses, saying, 'If, O chastiser of foes, thou dost not venture to fight with enemy, come thou and hold the reins of the steeds as I fight with the foe. Protected by the might of my arms, penetrate thou yon formidable and invincible array of cars guarded by heroic and mighty warriors. Fear not, O chastiser of foes, thou art a *Kshatriya* and the foremost of royal princes. Why dost thou, O tiger among men, succumb in the midst of the foe? I shall surely fight with the Kurus and recover the kine, penetrating into this formidable and inaccessible array of cars. Be thou my charioteer, O best of men, I will fight with the Kurus.' Thus speaking unto Uttara, the son of Virata, Vibhatsu, heretofore unconquered in battle, for a while comforted him. And then the son of Pritha, that foremost of smiters, raised on the car that fainting and reluctant prince stricken with fear!"

SECTION XXXIX

Vaisampayana said, "Beholding that bull among men seated on the car in the habit of a person of the third sex, driving toward the *Sami* tree, having taken (the flying) Uttara up, all the great car-warriors of the Kurus with Bhishma and Drona at their head, became affrighted at heart, suspecting the comer to be Dhananjaya. And seeing them so dispirited and marking also the many wonderful portents, that foremost of all wielders of arms, the preceptor Drona, son of Bharadwaja, said, 'Violent and hot are the winds that below, showering gravels in profusion. The sky also is overcast with a gloom of ashy hue. The clouds present the strange sight of being dry and waterless. Our weapons also of various kinds are coming out of their cases. The jackals are yelling hideously affrighted at the conflagrations on all sides. 41 The horses too are shedding tears, and our banners are trembling though moved by none. Such being the inauspicious indications seen, a great danger is at hand. Stay ye with vigilance. Protect ye your own selves and array the troops in order of battle. Stand ye, expecting a terrible slaughter, and guard ye well the kine. This mighty bowman, this foremost of all wielders of weapons, this hero that hath come in the habit of a person of the third sex, is the son of Pritha. There is no doubt of this.' Then addressing Bhishma, the preceptor continued, 'O offspring of the Ganges, apparelled as a woman, this is *Kiriti* called after a tree, the son of the enemy of the mountains, and having on his banner the sign of devastator of the gardens of Lanka's lord. Vanquishing us he will surely take away the kine today! 42 This chastiser of foes is the valiant son of Pritha surnamed *Savyasachin*. He doth not desist from conflict even with the gods and demons combined. Put to great hardship in the forest he cometh in wrath. Taught by even Indra himself, he is like unto Indra in battle. Therefore, ye Kauravas, I do not see any hero who can withstand him. It is said that the lord *Mahadeva* himself, disguised in the attire of a hunter, was gratified by this son of Pritha in battle on the mountains of Himavat.' Hearing these words, Karna said, 'You always censure us by speaking on the virtues of *Phalguna*. Arjuna, however, is not equal to even a full sixteenth part of myself or Duryodhana!' And Duryodhana said, 'If this be Partha, O Radheya, then my purpose hath already been fulfilled, for then, O king, if traced out, the Pandavas shall have to wander for twelve years again. Or, if this one be any other person in a eunuch's garb, I will soon prostrate him on the earth with keen-edged arrows.'"

Vaisampayana continued, "The son of Dhritarashtra, O chastiser of foes, having said this, Bhishma and Drona and Kripa and Drona's son all applauded his manliness!"

SECTION XL

Vaisampayana said, "Having reached that *Sami* tree, and having ascertained Virata's son to be exceedingly delicate and inexperienced in battle, Partha addressed him, saying, 'Enjoined by me, O Uttara, quickly take down (from this tree) some bows that are there. For these bows of thine are unable to bear my strength, my heavy weight when I shall grind down horses and elephants, and the stretch of my arms when I seek to vanquish the foe. Therefore, O Bhuminjaya, climb thou up this tree of thick foliage, for in this tree are tied the bows and arrows and banners and excellent coats of mail of the heroic sons of Pandu, viz., Yudhishthira and Bhima and Vibhatsu and the twins. There also is that bow of great energy, the *Gandiva* of Arjuna, which singly is equal to many thousands of other bows and which is capable of extending the limits of a kingdom. Large like a palmyra tree, able to bear the greatest stress, the largest of all weapons, capable of obstructing the foe, handsome, and smooth, and broad, without a knot, and adorned with gold, it is stiff and beautiful in make and beareth the heaviest weight. And the other bows also that are there, of Yudhishthira and Bhima and Vibhatsu and the twins, are equally mighty and tough.'"

SECTION XLI

"Uttara said, 'It hath been heard by us that a corpse is tied in this tree. How can I, therefore, being a prince by birth, touch it with my hands? Born in the *Kshatriya* order, and the son of a great king, and always observant of *mantras* and vows, it is not becoming of me to touch it. Why shouldst thou, O Vrihannala, make me a polluted and unclean bearer of corpses, by compelling me to come in contact with a corpse?'

"Vrihannala said, 'Thou shalt, O king of kings, remain clean and unpolluted. Do not fear, there are only bows in this tree and not corpses. Heir to the king of the Matsyas, and born in a noble family, why should I, O prince, make thee do such a reproachable deed?'"

Vaisampayana said, "Thus addressed by Partha, Virata's son, decked in ear-rings, alighted from the car, and climbed up that *Sami* tree reluctantly. And staying on the car, Dhananjaya, that slayer of enemies, said unto him, 'Speedily bring thou down those bows from the top of the tree.' And cutting off their wrappings first and then the ropes with which they were tied, the prince beheld the *Gandiva* there along with four other bows. And as they were untied, the splendour of those bows radiant as the sun, began to shine with great effulgence like unto that of the planets about the time of their rising. And beholding the forms of those bows, so like unto sighing snakes, he become afflicted with fear and in a moment the bristles of his body stood on their ends. And touching those large bows of great splendour, Virata's son, O king, thus spake unto Arjuna!"

SECTION XLII

"Uttara said, 'To what warrior of fame doth this excellent bow belong, on which are a hundred golden bosses and which hath such radiant ends? Whose is this excellent bow of good sides and easy hold, on the staff of which shine golden elephants of such brightness? Whose is this excellent bow, adorned with three scores of *Indragopakas* 43 of pure gold, placed on the back of the staff at proper intervals? Whose is this excellent bow, furnished with three golden suns of great effulgence, blazing forth with such brilliancy? Whose is this beautiful bow which is variegated with gold and gems, and on which are golden insects set with beautiful stones? Whose are these arrows furnished with wing around, numbering a thousand, having golden heads, and cased in golden quivers? Who owneth these large shafts, so thick, furnished with vulturine wings whetted on stone, yellowish in hue, sharp-pointed, well-tempered, and entirely made of iron? Whose is this sable quiver, 44 bearing five images of tigers, which holdeth shafts intermined with boar-eared arrows altogether numbering ten? Whose are these seven hundred arrows, long and thick, capable of drinking (the enemy's) blood, and looking like the crescent-shaped moon? 45 Whose are these gold-crested arrows whetted on stones, the lower halves of which are well-furnished with wings of the hue of parrots' feather and the upper halves, of well-tempered steels? 46 Whose is this excellent sword irresistible, and terrible to adversaries, with the mark of a toad on it, and pointed like a toad's head? 47 Cased in variegated sheath of tiger-skin, whose is this large sword of excellent blade and variegated with gold and furnished with tinkling bells? Whose is this handsome scimitar of polished blade and golden hilt? Manufactured in the country of the *Nishadas*, irresistible, incapable of being broken, whose is this sword of polished blade in a scabbard of cow-skin? Whose is this beautiful and long sword, sable in hue as the sky, mounted with gold, well-tempered, and cased in a sheath of goat-skin? Who owneth this heavy, well-tempered, and broad sword, just longer than the breadth of thirty fingers, polished by constant clash with other's weapons and kept in a case of gold, bright as fire? Whose is this beautiful scimitar of sable blade covered with golden bosses, capable of cutting through the bodies of adversaries, whose touch is as fatal as that of a venomous snake which is irresistible and exciteth the terror of foes? Asked by me, O Vrihannala, do thou answer me truly. Great is my wonder at the sight of all these excellent objects.'"

SECTION XLIII

"Vrihannala said, 'That about which thou hath first enquired is Arjuna's bow, of world-wide fame, called *Gandiva,* capable of devastating hostile hosts. Embellished with gold, this *Gandiva,* the highest and largest of all weapons belonged to Arjuna. Alone equal unto a hundred thousand weapons, and always capable of extending the confines of kingdoms, it is with this that Partha vanquisheth in battle both men and celestials. Worshipped ever by the gods, the *Danavas* and the *Gandharvas* and variegated with excellent colours, this large and smooth bow is without a knot or stain anywhere. Shiva held it first for a thousand years. Afterwards Prajapati held it for five hundred and three years. After that Sakra, for five and eighty years. And then Soma held it for five hundred years. And after that *Varuna* held it for a hundred years. And finally Partha, surnamed *Swetavahana,* 48 hath held it for five and sixty years. 49 Endued with great energy and of high celestial origin, this is the best of all bows. Adored among gods and men, it hath a handsome form. Partha obtained this beautiful bow from Varuna. This other bow of handsome sides and golden handle is Bhima's with which that son of Pritha, that chastiser of foes, had conquered the whole of the eastern regions. This other excellent bow of beautiful shape, adorned with images of *Indragopakas,* belongeth, O Virata's son, to king Yudhishthira. This other weapon with golden suns of blazing splendour shedding a dazzling effulgence around, belongeth to Nakula. And this bow adorned with golden images of insects and set also with gems and stones, belongeth to that son of Madri who is called Sahadeva. These winged arrows, thousand in number, sharp as razors and destructive as the poison of snakes, belong, O Virata's son, to Arjuna. When shooting them in battle against foes, these swift arrows blaze forth more brilliantly and become inexhaustible. And these long and thick shafts resembling the lunar crescent in shape, keen-edged and capable of thinning the enemy's ranks, belong to Bhima. And this quiver bearing five images of tigers, full of yellowish shafts whetted on stone and furnished with golden wings belong to Nakula. This is the quiver of the intelligent son of Madri, with which he had conquered in battle the whole of the western regions. And these arrows, all effulgent as the sun, painted all over with various colours, and capable of destroying enemies by thousands are those of Sahadeva. And these short and well-tempered and thick shafts, furnished with long feathers and golden heads, and consisting of three knots, belong to king Yudhishthira. And this sword with blade long and carved with the image of a toad and head shaped as a toad's mouth, strong and irresistible belongeth to Arjuna. Cased in a sheath of tiger-skin, of long blade, handsome and irresistible, and terrible to adversaries, this sword belongeth to Bhimasena. Of excellent blade and cased in a well-painted sheath, and furnished with a golden hilt, this handsome sword belongeth to the wise Kaurava—Yudhishthira the just. And this sword of strong blade, irresistible and intended for various excellent modes of fight and cased in a sheath of goat-skin, belongeth to Nakula. And this huge scimitar, cased in a sheath of cow-skin, strong and irresistible belongeth to Sahadeva.'"

SECTION XLIV

"Uttara said, 'Indeed, these weapons adorned with gold, belonging to the light-handed and high-souled Partha, look exceedingly beautiful. But where are that Arjuna, the son of Pritha, and Yudhishthira of the Kuru race, and Nakula, and Sahadeva, and Bhimasena, the sons of Pandu? Having lost their kingdom at dice, the high-souled Pandavas, capable of destroying all foes, are no longer heard of. Where also is Draupadi, the princess of *Panchala*, famed as the gem among women, who followed the sons of Pandu after their defeat at dice to the forest?'

"Arjuna said, 'I am Arjuna, called also Partha. Thy father's courtier is Yudhishthira and thy father's cook Vallava is Bhimasena, the groom of horses is Nakula, and Sahadeva is in the cow-pen. And know thou that the *Sairindhri* is Draupadi, for whose sake the Kichakas have been slain.'

"Uttara said, 'I would believe all this if thou canst enumerate the ten names of Partha, previously heard by me!'

"Arjuna said, 'I will, O son of Virata, tell thee my ten names. Listen thou and compare them with what thou hadst heard before. Listen to them with close attention and concentrated mind. They are *Arjuna, Phalguna, Jishnu, Kiritin, Swetavahana, Vibhatsu, Vijaya, Krishna, Savyasachin* and *Dhananjaya*.'

"Uttara said, 'Tell me truly why art thou called Vijaya, and why Swetavahana. Why art thou named Krishna and why Arjuna and Phalguna and Jishnu and Kiritin and Vibhatsu, and for what art thou Dhananjaya and Savyasachin? I have heard before about the origin of the several names of that hero, and can put faith in thy words if thou canst tell me all about them.'

"Arjuna said, 'They called me Dhananjaya because I lived in the midst of wealth, having subjugated all the countries and taking away their treasures. They called me Vijaya because when I go out to battle with invincible kings, I never return (from the field) without vanquishing them. I am called Swetavahana because when battling with the foe, white horses decked in golden armour are always yoked unto my car. They call me Phalguna because I was born on the breast of the Himavat on a day when the constellation *Uttara Phalguna* was on the ascendent. I am named

Kiritin from a diadem, resplendent like the sun, having been placed of old on my head by Indra during my encounter with the powerful *Danavas*. I am known as Vibhatsu among gods and men, for my never having committed a detestable deed on the battle-field. And since both of my hands are capable of drawing the *Gandiva*, I am known as Savyasachin among gods and men. They call me Arjuna because my complexion is very rare within the four boundaries of the earth and because also my acts are always stainless. I am known among human beings and celestials by the name of Jishnu, because I am unapproachable and incapable of being kept down, and a tamer of adversaries and son of the slayer of Paka. And Krishna, my tenth appellation, was given to me by my father out of affection towards his black-skinned boy of great purity.'"

Vaisampayana continued, "The son of Virata then, approaching nearer saluted Partha and said, 'My name is Bhuminjaya, and I am also called Uttara. It is by good luck, O Partha, that I behold thee. Thou art welcome, O Dhananjaya. O thou with red eyes, and arms that are mighty and each like unto the trunk of an elephant, it behoveth thee to pardon what I said unto thee from ignorance. And as wonderful and difficult have been the feats achieved by thee before, my fears have been dispelled, and indeed the love I bear to thee is great.'"

SECTION XLV

"Uttara said, 'O hero, mounting on this large car with myself as driver, which division of the (hostile) army wouldst thou penetrate? Commanded by thee, I would drive thee thither.'

"Arjuna said, 'I am pleased with thee, O tiger among men. Thou hast no cause of fear. I will rout all thy foes in battle, O great warrior, And, O thou of mighty arms, be at thy ease. Accomplishing great and terrible feats in the melee, I will fight with thy foes. Tie quickly all those quivers to my car, and take (from among those) a sword of polished blade and adorned with gold.'"

Vaisampayana continued, "Hearing these words of Arjuna, Uttara cast off all inactivity. And he speedily alighted from the tree, bringing with him Arjuna's weapons. Then Arjuna addressed him, saying, 'Yes, I will fight with the Kurus and recover thy kine. Protected by me, the top of this car will be to thee as a citadel. The passages and alleys and other divisions of this car will be the streets and edifices of that fortified city. These my arms will be its ramparts and gateways. This treble pole and my quiver will constitute defensive works inaccessible to the foe. This my banner—single and grand—will it not alone be equal unto those of thy city? This my bow-string will constitute the catapults and cannons for vomiting forth missiles on the besieging host. My excited wrath will make that fortress formidable, and the clatter of my car-wheels—will it not resemble the kettle-drums of thy capital? Ridden by myself wielding the *Gandiva*, this car will be incapable of being vanquished by the hostile host, O son of Virata, let thy fear be dispelled.'

"Uttara said, 'I am no longer afraid of these. I know thy steadiness in battle, which is even like unto that of Kesava or Indra himself. But reflecting on this, I am continually bewildered. Foolish as I am, I am incapable of arriving at certain conclusion. By what distressful circumstances could *a person of such handsome limbs and auspicious signs become deprived of manhood*? Indeed, thou seemest to me to be Mahadeva, or Indra, or the chief of the Gandharvas, dwelling in the guise only of one of the third sex.'

"Arjuna said, 'I tell thee truly that I am only observing this vow for a whole year agreeable to the behest of my elder brother. O thou of mighty arms, I am not truly one of the neuter sex, but I have adopted this vow of eunuchism from subservience to another's will and from desire of religious merit. O prince, know me now to have completed my vow.'

"Uttara said, 'Thou hast conferred a great favour on me today, for I now find that my suspicion was not altogether unfounded. Indeed, such a person as thou, O best of men, cannot be of the neuter sex. I have now an ally in battle. I can now fight with the celestials themselves. My fears have been dispelled. What shall I do? Command me now. Trained in driving cars by a learned preceptor I will, O bull among men, hold the reins of thy horses that are capable of breaking the ranks of hostile cars. Know me, O bull among men, to be as competent a charioteer as Daruka of Vasudeva, or Matali of Sakra. The horse that is yoked unto the right-hand pole (of thy car) and whose hoofs as they light on the ground are scarcely visible when running, is like unto *Sugriva* of Krishna. This other handsome horse, the foremost of his race, that is yoked unto the left pole, is, I regard, equal in speed to *Meghapushpa*. This (third) beautiful horse, clad in golden mail, yoked unto the rear-pole on the left, is, I regard, *Sivya* equal in speed to but superior in strength. And this (fourth) horse, yoked to the rear-pole on the right, is regarded as superior to *Valahaka* in speed and strength. This car is worthy of bearing on the field of battle a bowman like thee, and thou also art worthy of fighting on this car. This is what I think!'"

Vaisampayana continued, "Then Arjuna, endued with great energy, took off the bracelets from his arms and wore on his hands a pair of beautiful gloves embroidered with gold. And he then tied his black and curling locks with a piece of white cloth. And seated on that excellent car with face turned to the east, the mighty-armed hero, purifying his body and concentrating his soul, recalled to his mind all his weapons. And all the weapons came, and addressing the royal son of Partha, said, 'We are here, O illustrious one. We are thy servants, O son of Indra.' And bowing unto them, Partha received them unto his hands and replied unto them, saying, 'Dwell ye all in my memory.' And obtaining all his weapons, the hero looked cheerful. And quickly stringing his bow, the *Gandiva*, he twanged it. And the twang of that bow was as loud as the collision of two mighty bulls. And dreadful was the sound that filled the earth, and violent was the wind that blew on all sides. And thick was the shower of fallen meteors 50 and all sides were enveloped in gloom. And the birds began to totter in the skies and large trees began to shake. 51 And loud as the burst of the thunder, the Kurus knew from that sound that it was Arjuna that drew with his hands the string of his best of bows from his car. And Uttara said, 'Thou, O best of Pandavas, art alone. These mighty car-warriors are many. How wilt thou vanquish in battle all these that are skilled in every kind of weapon? Thou, O son of Kunti, art without a follower, while the Kauravas have many. It is for this, O thou of mighty arms, that I stay beside thee, stricken with fear.' Bursting out into loud laughter, Partha said unto him, 'Be not afraid, O hero, what friendly follower had I while fighting with the mighty *Gandharvas* on the occasion of the *Ghoshayatra*? Who was my ally while engaged in the terrific conflict at *Khandava* against so many celestials and *Danavas*? Who was my ally when I fought, on behalf of the lord of the celestials against the mighty *Nivatakavachas* and the *Paulomas*! And who was my ally, O child, while I encountered in battle innumerable kings at the *Swayamvara* to the princess of Panchala? Trained in arms by the preceptor Drona, by Sakra, and Vaisravana, and Yama, and Varuna, and Agni, and Kripa, and Krishna of Madhu's race, and by the wielder of the *Pinaka* (Siva), why shall I not fight with these? Drive thou my car speedily, and let thy heart's fever be dispelled.'"

SECTION XLVI

Vaisampayana said, "Making Uttara his charioteer, and circumambulating the *Sami* tree, the son of Pandu set out taking all his weapons with him. And that mighty car-warrior set out with Uttara as the driver of his car, having taken down that banner with the lion's figure and deposited it at the foot of the *Sami* tree. And he hoisted on that car his own golden banner bearing the figure of an ape with a lion's tail, which was a celestial illusion contrived by Viswakarman himself. For, as soon, indeed, as he had thought of that gift of Agni, than the latter, knowing his wish, ordered those superhuman creatures (that usually sat there) to take their place in that banner. And furnished with a beautiful flag of handsome make, with quivers attached to it, and adorned with gold, that excellent flag-staff of celestial beauty then quickly fell from the firmament on his car.
52 And beholding that banner arrived on his car, the hero circumambulated it (respectively). And then the ape-bannered Vibhatsu, the son of Kunti, called also Swetavahana, with fingers cased in leathern fences of the *Iguana* skin, and taking up his bow and arrows set out in a northernly direction. And that grinder of foes, possessed of great strength, then forcibly blew his large conch-shell, of thundering sound, capable of making the bristles of foes to stand on their ends. And at the sound of that conch, those steeds endued with swiftness dropped down on the ground on their knees. And Uttara also, greatly affrighted, sat down on the car. And thereupon the son of Kunti took the reins himself and raising the steeds, placed them in their proper positions. And embracing Uttara, he encouraged him also, saying, 'Fear not, O foremost of princes, thou art, O chastiser of foes, a *Kshatriya* by birth. Why, O tiger among men, dost thou become so dispirited in the midst of foes? Thou must have heard before the blare of many conchs and the note of many trumpets, and the roar also of many elephants in the midst of ranks arrayed for battled. Why art thou, therefore, so dispirited and agitated and terrified by the blare of this conch, as if thou wert an ordinary person?'

"Uttara said, 'Heard have I the blare of many a conch and many a trumpet and the roar of many an elephant stationed in the battle-array, but never have I heard before the blare of such conch. Nor have I ever seen a banner like this. Never before have I heard also the twang of a bow such as this. Truly, sir, with the blare of this conch, the twang of this bow, the superhuman cries of the creatures stationed on this banner, and the battle of this car, my mind is greatly bewildered. My perception of the directions also is confused, and my heart is painfully afflicted. The whole firmament seemeth to me to have been covered by this banner, and everything seemeth to be hidden from my view! My ears also have been deafened by the twang of the *Gandiva*!' 53

"Arjuna said, 'Firmly stand thou on the car, pressing thy feet on it, and tightly catch hold of the bridles, for I will blow the conch again.'"

Vaisampayana said, "Arjuna then blew his conch again, that conch which filled foes with grief and enhanced the joy of friends. And the sound was so loud that it seemed to split hills and mountains, and pierce mountain-caves and the cardinal points. And Uttara once again sat down on the car, clinging to it in fear. And with the blare of the conch and the rattle of the car-wheels, and the twang of the Gandiva, the earth itself seemed to tremble. And beholding Uttara's fight, Dhananjaya began to comfort him again.'

"Meanwhile, Drona said, 'From the rattle of the car, and from the manner in which the clouds have enveloped the sky and the earth itself trembles, this warrior can be none else than *Savyasachin*. Our weapons do not shine, our steeds are dispirited, and our fires, though fed with fuel, do not blare up. All this is ominous. All our animals are setting up a frightful howl, gazing towards the sun. The crows are perching on our banners. All this is ominous. Yon vultures and kites on our right portend a great danger. That jackal also, running through our ranks, waileth dismally. Lo, it hath escaped unstruck. All this portends a heavy calamity. The bristles also of ye all are on their ends. Surely, this forebodes a great destruction of Kshatriyas in battle. Things endued with light are all pale; beasts and birds look fierce; and there are to be witnessed many terrific portents indicative of the destruction of Kshatriyas. And these omens forebode great havoc among ourselves. O king, thy ranks seem to be confounded by these blazing meteors, and thy animals look dispirited and seem to be weeping. Vultures and kites are wheeling all around thy troops. Thou shalt have to repent upon beholding thy army afflicted by Partha's arrows. Indeed, our ranks seem to have been already vanquished, for none is eager to go to fight. All our warriors are of pale face, and almost deprived of their senses. Sending the kine ahead we should stand here, ready to strike, with all our warriors arrayed in order of battle.'"

SECTION XLVII

Vaisampayana said, "King Duryodhana then, on the field of battle said unto Bhishma, and unto Drona—that tiger among warriors, and unto Kripa—that mighty car-warrior, these words, 'Both myself and Karna had said this unto the preceptors. 54 I refer to the subject again, for I am not satisfied with having said it once. Even this was the pledge of the sons of Pandu that if defeated (at dice) they would reside to our knowledge in countries and woods for twelve years, and one more year unknown to us. That thirteenth year, instead of being over, is yet running. Vibhatsu, therefore, who is still to live undiscovered hath appeared before us. And if Vibhatsu hath come before the term of exile is at end, the Pandavas shall have to pass another twelve years in the woods. Whether it is due to forgetfulness (on their part) induced by desire of dominion, or whether it is a mistake of ours, it behoveth Bhishma to calculate the shortness or excess (of the promised period). When an object of desire may or may not be attained, a doubt necessarily attaches to one of the alternatives, and what is decided in one way often ends differently. 55 Even moralists are puzzled in judging of their own acts. 56 As regards ourselves, we have come hither to fight with the Matsyas and to seize their kine stationed towards the north. If, meanwhile, it is Arjuna that hath come, what fault can attach to us? We have come hither to fight against the Matsyas on behalf of the Trigartas; and as numerous were the acts represented unto us of the oppressions committed by the Matsyas, it was for this that we promised aid to the Trigartas who were overcome with fear. And it was agreed between us that they should first seize, on the afternoon of the seventh lunar day, the enormous wealth of kine that the Matsyas have, and that we should, at sunrise of the eighteen day of the moon, seize these kine when the king of the Matsyas would be pursuing those first seized. It may be that the Trigartas are now bringing away the kine, or being defeated, are coming towards us for negotiating with the king of the Matsyas. Or, it may be, that having driven the Trigartas off, the king of the Matsyas, at the head of this people and his whole army of fierce warriors, appeareth on the scene and advanceth to make night-attacks upon us. It may be that some one leader among them, endued with mighty energy, is advancing for vanquishing us, or, it may be that the king himself of the Matsyas is come. But be it the king of the Matsyas or Vibhatsu, we must all fight him. Even this hath been our pledge. Why are all these of foremost car-warriors,—Bhishma and Drona and Kripa and Vikarna and Drona's son,—now sitting on their cars, panic-stricken? At present there is nothing better than fighting. Therefore, make up your minds. If, for the cattle we have seized, an encounter takes place with the divine wielder himself of the thunderbolt or even with Yama, who is there that will be liable to reach Hastinapura? Pierced by the shafts (of the foe), how will the foot-soldiers, in flying through the deep forest with their backs on the field, escape with life, when escape for the cavalry is doubtful?' Hearing these words of Duryodhana, Karna said, 'Disregarding the preceptor, make all arrangements. He knoweth well the intentions of the Pandavas and striketh terror in our hearts. I see that his affection for Arjuna is very great. Seeing him only coming, he chanteth his praises. Make ye such arrangements that our troops may not break. Everything is in confusion for Drona's having only heard the neigh of (Arjuna's) steeds. Make ye such arrangements that these troops, come to a distant land in this hot season and in the midst of this mighty forest, may not fall into confusion and be subjugated by the foe. The Pandavas are always the special favourites of the preceptor. The selfish Pandavas have stationed Drona amongst us. Indeed, he betrayeth himself by his speech. Who would ever extol a person upon hearing the neigh only of his steeds? Horses always neigh, whether walking or standing, the winds blow at all times; and Indra also always showereth rain. The roar of the clouds may frequently be heard. What hath Partha to do with these, and why is he to be praised for these? All this (on Drona's part), therefore, is due only to either the desire of doing good to Arjuna or to his wrath and hatred towards us. Preceptors are wise, and sinless, and very kind to all creatures. They, however, should never be consulted at times of peril. It is in luxurious palaces, and assemblies and pleasure-gardens, that learned men, capable of making speeches, seem to be in their place. Performing many wonderful things, in the assembly, it is there that learned men find their place, or even there where sacrificial utensils and their proper placing and washing are needed. In a knowledge of the lapses of others, in studying the characters of men, in the science of horses and elephants and cars, in treating the diseases of asses and camels and goats and sheeps and kine, in planning buildings and gateways, and in pointing out the defects of food and drink, the learned are truly in their own sphere. Disregarding learned men that extol the heroism of the foe, make ye such arrangements that the foe may be destroyed. Placing the kine securely, array the troops in order of battle. Place guards in proper places so that we may fight the foe.'"

SECTION XLVIII

"Karna said, 'I behold all these blessed ones, looking as if alarmed and panic-struck and unresolved and unwilling to fight. If he that is come is the king of the Matsyas or Vibhatsu, even I will resist him as the banks resist the swelling sea. Shot from my bow these straight and flying arrows, like gliding snakes, are all sure of aim. Discharged by my light hands, these keen-edged arrows furnished with golden wings shall cover Partha all over, like locusts shrouding a tree. Strongly pressed by these winged arrows, the bow-string will cause these my leathern fences to produce sounds that will be heard to resemble those of a couple of kettle-drums. Having been engaged in ascetic austerities for the (last) eight and five years, Vibhatsu will strike me but mildly in this conflict, and the son of Kunti having become a Brahmana endued with good qualities, hath thus become a fit person to quietly receive shafts by thousands shot by me. This mighty bowman is indeed, celebrated over the three worlds. I, too, am, by no means, inferior to Arjuna, that foremost of human beings. With golden arrows furnished with vulturine wings shot on all sides, let the firmament seem today to swarm with fire-flies. Slaying Arjuna in battle, I will discharge today that debt, difficult of repayments, but promised of old by me unto Dhritarashtra's son. When man is there, even amongst all the gods and the *Asuras*, that will endure to stand in the teeth of the straight arrows shot from my bow? Let my flying arrows, winged and depressed at the middle, present the spectacle of the coursing of the fire-flies through the welkin. Hard though he be as Indra's thunderbolt and possessed of the energy of the chief of the celestials, I will surely grind Partha, even as one afflicts an elephant by means of burning brands. A heroic and mighty car-warrior as he is, and the foremost of all wielders of weapons I shall seize the unresisting Partha, even like Garuda seizing a snake. Irresistible like fire, and fed by the fuel of swords, darts, and arrows, the blazing Pandava-fire that consumeth foes, will be extinguished even by myself who am like unto a mighty cloud incessantly dropping an arrowy shower,—the multitude of cars (I will lead) constituting its thunder, and the speed of my horses, the wind in advance. Discharged from my bow, my arrows like venomous snakes will pierce Partha's body, like serpent penetrating through an ant-hill. Pierced with well-tempered and straight shafts endued with golden wings and great energy, behold ye today the son of Kunti decked like a hill covered with *Karnikara* flowers. Having obtained weapons from that best of ascetics—the son of Jamadagni, I would, relying on their energy, fight with even the celestials. Struck with my javelin, the ape stationed on his banner-top shall fall down today on the ground, uttering terrible cries. The firmament will today be filled with the cries of the (superhuman) creatures stationed in the flagstaff of the foe, and afflicted by me, they will fly away in all directions. I shall today pluck up by the roots the long-existing dart in Duryodhana's heart by throwing Arjuna down from his car. The Kauravas will today behold Partha with his car broken, his horses killed, his valour gone, and himself sighing like a snake. Let the Kauravas, following their own will go away taking this wealth of kine, or, if they wish, let them stay on their cars and witness my combat.'"

SECTION XLIX

"Kripa said, 'O Radheya, thy crooked heart always inclineth to war. Thou knowest not the true nature of things; nor dost thou take into account their after-consequences. There are various kinds of expedients inferrable from the scriptures. Of these, a battle hath been regarded by those acquainted with the past, as the most sinful. It is only when time and place are favourable that military operations can lead to success. In the present instance, however, the time being unfavourable, no good results will be deprived. A display of prowess in proper time and place becometh beneficial. It is by the favourableness or otherwise (of time and place) that the opportuneness of an act is determined. Learned men can never act according to the ideas of a car-maker. Considering all this, an encounter with Partha is not advisible for us. Alone he saved the Kurus (from the *Gandharvas*), and alone he satiated Agni. Alone he led the life of a *Brahmacharin* for five years (on the breast of Himavat). Taking up Subhadra on his car, alone he challenged Krishna to single combat. Alone he fought with Rudra who stood before him as a forester. It was in this very forest that Partha rescued Krishna while she was being taken away (by Jayadratha). It is he alone that hath, for five years, studied the science of weapons under Indra. Alone vanquishing all foes he hath spread the fame of the Kurus. Alone that chastiser of foes vanquished in battle Chitrasena, the king of the *Gandharvas* and in a moment his invincible troops also. Alone he overthrew in battle the fierce *Nivatakavachas* and the *Kalakhanchas*, that were both incapable of being slain by the gods themselves. What, however, O Karna, hath been achieved by thee single-handed like any of the sons of Pandu, each of whom had alone subjugated many lords of earth? Even Indra himself is unfit to encounter Partha in battle. He, therefore, that desireth to fight with Arjuna should take a sedative. As to thyself, thou desirest to take out the fangs of an angry snake of virulent poison by stretching forth thy right hand and extending thy forefinger. Or, wandering alone in the forest thou desirest to ride an infuriate elephant and go to a boar without a hook in hand. Or, rubbed over with clarified butter and dressed in silken robes, thou desirest to pass through the midst of a blazing fire fed with fat and tallow and clarified butter. Who is there that would, binding his own hands and feet and tying a huge stone unto his neck, cross the ocean swimming with his bare arms? What manliness is there in such an act? O Karna, he is a fool that would, without skill in weapons and without strength, desire to fight with Partha who is so mighty and skilled in weapons. Dishonestly deceived by us and liberated from thirteen years' exile, will not the illustrious hero annihilate us? Having ignorantly come to a place where Partha lay concealed like fire hidden in a well, we have, indeed, exposed to a great danger. But irresistible though he be in battle, we should fight against him. Let, therefore, our troops, clad in mail, stand here arrayed in ranks and ready to strike. Let Drona and Duryodhana and Bhishma and thyself and Drona's son and ourselves, all fight with the son of Pritha. Do not, O Karna, act so rashly as to fight alone. If we six car-warriors be united, we can then be a match for and fight with that son of Pritha who is resolved to fight and who is as fierce as the wielder of the thunderbolt. Aided by our troops arrayed in ranks, ourselves—great bowmen—standing carefully will fight with Arjuna even as the *Danavas* encounter Vasava in battle.'"

SECTION L

"Aswatthaman said, 'The kine, O Karna, have not yet been won, nor have they yet crossed the boundary (of their owner's dominions), nor have they yet reached Hastinapura. Why dost thou, therefore, boast of thyself? Having won numerous battles, and acquired enormous wealth, and vanquished hostile hosts, men of true heroism speak not a word of their prowess. Fire burneth mutely and mutely doth the sun shine. Mutely also doth the Earth bear creatures, both mobile and immobile. The Self-existent hath sanctioned such offices for the four orders that having recourse to them each may acquire wealth without being censurable. A Brahmana, having studied the *Vedas*, should perform sacrifices himself, and officiate at the sacrifices of others. And a Kshatriya, depending upon the bow, should perform sacrifices himself but should never officiate at the sacrifices of others. And a Vaisya, having earned wealth, should cause the rites enjoined in the *Vedas* to be performed for himself. A Sudra should always wait upon and serve the other three orders. As regards those that live by practising the profession of flowers and vendors of meat, they may earn wealth by expedients fraught with deceit and fraud. Always acting according to the dictates of the scriptures, the exalted sons of Pandu acquired the sovereignty of the whole earth, and they always act respectfully towards their superiors, even if the latter prove hostile to them. What Kshatriya is there that expressed delight at having obtained a kingdom by means of dice, like this wicked and shameless son of Dhritarashtra? Having acquired wealth in this way by deceit and fraud like a vendor of meat, who that is wise boast of it? In what single combat didst thou vanquish Dhananjaya, or Nakula, or Sahadeva, although thou hast robbed them of their wealth? In what battle didst thou defeat Yudhishthira, or Bhima that foremost of strong men? In what battle was Indraprastha conquered by thee? What thou hast done, however, O thou of wicked deeds, is to drag that princess to court while she was ill and had but one raiment on? Thou hast cut the mighty root, delicate as the sandal, of the Pandava tree. Actuated by desire of wealth, when thou madest the Pandavas act as slaves, rememberest thou what Vidura said! We see that men and others, even insects and ants, show forgiveness according to their power of endurance. The son of Pandu, however, is incapable of forgiving the sufferings of Draupadi. Surely, Dhananjaya cometh here for the destruction of the sons of Dhritarashtra. It is true, affecting great wisdom, thou art for making speeches but will not Vibhatsu, that slayer of foes, exterminate us all! If it be gods, or *Gandharvas* or *Asuras*, or *Rakshasas*, will Dhananjaya the son of Kunti, desist to fight from panic? Inflamed with wrath upon whomsoever he will fall, even him he will overthrow like a tree under the weight of Garuda! Superior to thee in prowess, in bowmanship equal unto the lord himself of the celestials, and in battle equal unto Vasudeva himself, who is there that would not praise Partha? Counteracting celestial weapons with celestial, and human weapons with human, what man is a match for Arjuna? Those acquainted with the scriptures declare that a disciple is no way inferior to a son, and it is for this that the son of Pandu is a favourite of Drona. Employ thou the means now which thou hadst adopted in the match at dice,—the same means, viz., by which thou hadst subjugated Indraprastha, and the same means by which thou hadst dragged Krishna to the assembly! This thy wise uncle, fully conversant with the duties of the *Kshatriya* order—this deceitful gambler Sakuni, the prince of Gandhara, let *him* fight now! The *Gandiva,* however, doth not cast dice such as the *Krita* or the *Dwapara,* but it shooteth upon foes blazing and keen-edged shafts by myriads. The fierce arrows shot from the *Gandiva,* endued with great energy and furnished with vulturine wings, car, pierce even mountains. The destroyer of all, named Yama, and Vayu, and the horse-faced Agni, leave some remnant behind, but Dhananjaya inflamed with wrath never doth so. As thou hadst, aided by thy uncle, played at dice in the assembly so do fight in this battle protected by Suvala's son. Let the preceptor, if he chooses fight; I shall not, however, fight with Dhananjaya. We are to fight with the king of the Matsyas, if indeed, he cometh in the track of the kine.'"

SECTION LI

"Bhishma said, 'Drona's son observeth well, and Kripa too observeth rightly. As for Karna, it is only out of regard for the duties of the Kshatriya order that he desireth to fight. No man of wisdom can blame the preceptor. I, however, am of opinion that fight we must, considering both the time and the place. Why should not that man be bewildered who hath five adversaries effulgent as five suns, who are heroic combatants and who have just emerged from adversity? Even those conversant with morality are bewildered in respect of their own interests. It is for this, O king, that I tell thee this, whether my words be acceptable to you or not. What Karna said unto thee was only for raising our (drooping) courage. As regards thyself, O preceptor's son, forgive everything. The business at hand is very grave. When the son of Kunti hath come, this is not the time for quarrel. Everything should now be forgiven by thyself and the preceptor Kripa. Like light in the sun, the mastery of all weapons doth reside in you. As beauty is never separated from *Chandramas*, so are the *Vedas* and the *Brahma* weapon both established in you. It is often seen that the four *Vedas* dwell in one object and *Kshatriya* attributes in another. We have never heard of these two dwelling together in any other person than the preceptor of the Bharata race and his son. Even this is what I think. In the *Vedantas*, in the *Puranas*, and in old histories, who save Jamadagni, O king, would be Drona's superior? A combination of the *Brahma* weapon with the *Vedas*,—this is never to be seen anywhere else. O preceptor's son, do thou forgive. This is not the time for disunion. Let all of us, uniting, fight with Indra's son who hath come. Of all the calamities that may befall an army that have been enumerated by men of wisdom, the worst is disunion among the leaders.' Aswatthaman said, 'O bull among men, these thy just observations, need not be uttered in our presence; the preceptor, however, filled with wrath, had spoken of Arjuna's virtues. The virtues of even an enemy should be admitted, while the faults of even one's preceptor may be pointed out; therefore one should, to the best of his power, declare the merits of a son or a disciple.'

"Duryodhana said, 'Let the preceptor grant his forgiveness and let peace be restored. If the preceptor be at one with us, whatever should be done (in view of the present emergency) would seem to have been already done.'"

Vaisampayana continued, "Then, O Bharata, Duryodhana assisted by Karna and Kripa, and the high-souled Bhishma pacified Drona.

"Drona said, 'Appeased I have already been at the words first spoken by Bhishma, the son of Santanu. Let such arrangements be made that Partha may not be able to approach Duryodhana in battle. And let such arrangements be made that king Duryodhana may not be captured by the foe, in consequence either of his rashness or want of judgment. Arjuna hath not, to be sure, revealed himself before the expiry of the term of exile. Nor will he pardon this act (of ours) today, having only recovered the kine. Let such arrangements, therefore, be made that he may not succeed in attacking Dhritarashtra's son and defeating our troops. Like myself (who am doubtful of the completion of period of exile) Duryodhana also had said so before. Bearing it in mind, it behoveth the son of Ganga to say what is true.'"

SECTION LII

"Bhishma said, 'The wheel of time revolves with its divisions, viz., with *Kalas* and *Kasthas* and *Muhurtas* and days and fortnights and months and constellations and planets and seasons and years. In consequence of their fractional excesses and the deviations of also of the heavenly bodies, there is an increase of two months in every five years. It seems to me that calculating this wise, there would be an excess of five months and twelve nights in thirteen years. Everything, therefore, that the sons of Pandu had promised, hath been exactly fulfilled by them. Knowing this to be certain, Vibhatsu hath made his appearance. All of them are high-souled and fully conversant with the meanings of the scriptures. How would they deviate from virtue that have Yudhishthira for their guide? The sons of Kunti do not yield to temptation. They have achieved a difficult feat. If they had coveted the possession of their kingdom by unfair means, then those descendants of the Kuru race would have sought to display their prowess at the time of the match at dice. Bound in bonds of virtue, they did not deviate from the duties of the Kshatriya order. He that will regard them to have behaved falsely will surely meet with defeat. The sons of Pritha would prefer death to falsehood. When the time, however, comes, those bulls among men—the Pandavas—endued with energy like that of Sakra, would not give up what is theirs even if it is defended by the wielder himself of the thunderbolt. We shall have to oppose in battle the foremost of all wielders of weapons. Therefore, let such advantageous arrangements as have the sanction of the good and the honest be now made without loss of time so that our possessions may not be appropriated by the foe. O king of kings, O Kaurava, I have never seen a battle in which one of the parties could say,—*we are sure to win*. When a battle occurs, there must be victory or defeat, prosperity or adversity. Without doubt, a party to a battle must have either of the two. Therefore, O king of kings, whether a battle be now proper or not consistent with virtue or not, make thy arrangements soon, for Dhananjaya is at hand.'

"Duryodhana said, 'I will not, O grandsire, give back the Pandavas their kingdom. Let every preparation, therefore, for battle be made without delay.'

"Bhishma said, 'Listen to what I regard as proper, if it pleases thee. I should always say what is for thy good, O Kaurava. Proceed thou towards the capital, without loss of time, taking with thee a fourth part of the army. And let another fourth march, escorting the kine. With half the troops we will fight the Pandava. Myself and Drona, and Karna and Aswatthaman and Kripa will resolutely withstand Vibhatsu, or the king of the Matsyas, or Indra himself, if he approaches. Indeed, we will withstand any of these like the bank withstanding the surging sea.'"

Vaisampayana continued, "These words spoken by the high-souled Bhishma were acceptable to them, and the king of the Kauravas acted accordingly without delay. And having sent away the king and then the kine, Bhishma began to array the soldiers in order of battle. And addressing the preceptor, he said, 'O preceptor, stand thou in the centre, and let Aswatthaman stand on the left, and let the wise Kripa, son of Saradwata, defend the right wing, and let Karna of the *Suta* caste, clad in mail, stand in the van. I will stand in the rear of the whole army, protecting it from that point.'"

SECTION LIII

Vaisampayana said, "After the Kauravas, O Bharata, had taken their stand in this order, Arjuna, filling the air with the rattle and din of his car, advanced quickly towards them. And the Kurus beheld his banner-top and heard the rattle and din of his car as also the twang of the *Gandiva* stretched repeatedly by him. And noting all this, and seeing that great car-warrior—the wielder of the *Gandiva*—come, Drona spoke thus, 'That is the banner-top of Partha which shineth at a distance, and this is the noise of his car, and that is the ape that roareth frightfully. Indeed, the ape striketh terror in the troops. And there stationed on that excellent car, the foremost of car-warriors draweth that best of bows, the *Gandiva,* whose twang is as loud as the thunder. Behold, these two shafts coming together fall at my feet, and two others pass off barely touching my ears. Completing the period of exile and having achieved many wonderful feats, Partha saluteth me and whispereth in my ears. Endued with wisdom and beloved of his relatives, this Dhananjaya, the son of Pandu, is, indeed, beheld by us after a long time, blazing with beauty and grace. Possessed of car and arrows, furnished with handsome fences and quiver and conch and banner and coat of mail, decked with diadem and scimitar and bow, the son of Pritha shineth like the blazing (*Homa*) fire surrounded with sacrificial ladles and fed with sacrificial butter.'"

Vaisampayana continued, "Beholding the Kurus ready for battle, Arjuna addressing Matsya's son in words suitable to the occasion, said, 'O charioteer, restrain thou the steeds at such a point whence my arrows may reach the enemy. Meanwhile, let me see, where, in the midst of this army, is that vile wretch of the Kuru race. Disregarding all these, and singling out that vainest of princes I will fall upon his head, for upon the defeat of that wretch the others will regard themselves as defeated. There standeth Drona, and thereafter him his son. And there are those great bowmen—Bhishma and Kripa and Karna. I do not see, however, the king there. I suspect that anxious to save his life, he retreateth by the southern road, taking away with him the kine. Leaving this array of car-warriors, proceed to the spot where Suyodhana is. There will I fight, O son of Virata, for there the battle will not be fruitless, Defeating him I will come back, taking away the kine.'"

Vaisampayana continued, "Thus addressed, the son of Virata restrained the steeds with an effort and turned them by a pull at the bridle from the spot where those bulls of the Kuru race were, and urged them on towards the place where Duryodhana was. And as Arjuna went away leaving that thick array of cars, Kripa, guessing his intention, addressed his own comrades, saying, 'This Vibhatsu desireth not to take up his stand at a spot remote from the king. Let us quickly fall upon the flanks of the advancing hero. When inflamed with wrath, none else, unassisted, can encounter him in battle save the deity of a thousand eyes, or Krishna the son of Devaki. Of what use to us would the kine be or this vast wealth also, if Duryodhana were to sink, like a boat, in the ocean of *Partha*?' Meanwhile, Vibhatsu, having proceeded towards that division of the army, announced himself speedily by name, and covered the troops with his arrows thick as locusts. And covered with those countless shafts shot by Partha, the hostile warriors could not see anything, the earth itself and the sky becoming overwhelmed therewith. And the soldiers who had been ready for the fight were so confounded that none could even the flee from the field. And beholding the light-handedness of Partha they all applauded it mentally. And Arjuna then blew his conch which always made the bristles of the foe stand erect. And twanging his best of bows, he urged the creatures on his flagstaff to roar more frightfully. And at the blare of his conch and the rattle of his car-wheels, and the twang of the *Gandiva*, and the roar of the superhuman creatures stationed on his flagstaff, the earth itself began to tremble. And shaking their upraised tails and lowing together, the kine turned back, proceeding along the southern road.'"

SECTION LIV

Vaisampayana said, "Having disorganised the hostile host by force and having recovered the kine, that foremost of bowmen, desirous of fighting again, proceeded towards Duryodhana. And beholding the kine running wild towards the city of the Matsyas, the foremost warriors of the Kurus regarded Kiritin to have already achieved success. And all of a sudden they fell upon Arjuna who was advancing towards Duryodhana. And beholding their countless divisions firmly arrayed in order of battle with countless banners waving over them, that slayer of foes, addressing the son of the king of the Matsyas, said, 'Urge on, to the best of their speed by this road, these white steeds decked with golden bridles. Strive thou well, for I would approach this crowd of Kuru lions. Like an elephant desiring an encounter with another, the *Suta's* son of wicked soul eagerly desireth a battle with me. Take me, O prince, to him who hath grown so proud under the patronage of Duryodhana.' Thus addressed, the son of Virata by means of those large steeds endued with the speed of the wind and furnished with golden armour, broke that array of cars and took the Pandava into the midst of the battle-field. And seeing this those mighty car-warriors, Chitrasena and Sangramajit and Satrusaha and Jaya, desirous of aiding Karna, rushed with arrows and long shafts, towards the advancing hero of Bharata's race. Then that foremost of men, inflamed with wrath, began to consume by means of fiery arrows shot from his bow, that array of cars belonging to those bulls among the Kurus, like a tremendous conflagration consuming a forest. Then, when the battle began to rage furiously, the Kuru hero, Vikarna, mounted on his car, approached that foremost of car-warriors, Partha, the younger brother of Bhima,—showering upon him terrible shafts thick and long. Then cutting Vikarna's bow furnished with a tough string and horns overlaid with gold, Arjuna cut off his flagstaff. And Vikarna, beholding his flagstaff cut off, speedily took to flight. And after Vikarna's flight, Satruntapa, unable to repress his ire, began to afflict Partha, that obstructer of foes and achiever of super-human feats, by means of a perfect shower of arrows. And drowned, as it were, in the midst of the Kuru-array, Arjuna, pierced by that mighty car-warrior,—king Satruntapa—pierced the latter in return with five and then slew his car-driver with ten shafts, and pierced by that bull of the Bharata race with an arrow capable of cleaving the thickest coat of mail, Satruntapa fell dead on the field of battle, like a tree from a mountain-top torn up by the wind. And those brave bulls among men, mangled in battle by that braver bull among men, began to waver and tremble like mighty forests shaken by the violence of the wind that blows at the time of the universal dissolution. And struck in battle by Partha, the son of Vasava, those well-dressed heroes among men—those givers of wealth endued with the energy of Vasava—defeated and deprived of life, began to measure their lengths on the ground, like full-grown Himalayan elephants clad in mails of black steel decked with gold. And like unto a raging fire consuming a forest at the close of summer, that foremost of men, wielding the *Gandiva*, ranged the field in all directions, slaying his foes in battle thus. And as the wind rangeth at will, scattering masses of clouds and fallen leaves in the season of spring, so did that foremost of car-warriors—Kiritin—ranged in that battle, scattering all his foes before him. And soon slaying the red steeds yoked unto the car of Sangramajit, the brother of Vikartana's son, that hero decked in diadem and endued with great vigour then cut off his antagonist's head by a crescent-shaped arrow. And when his brother was slain, Vikartana's son of the *Suta* caste, mustering all his prowess, rushed at Arjuna, like a huge elephant with out-stretched tusks, or like a tiger at a mighty bull. And the son of Vikarna quickly pierced the son of Pandu with twelve shafts and all his steeds also in every part of their bodies and Virata's son too in his hand. And rushing impetuously against Vikarna's son who was suddenly advancing against him, Kiritin attacked him fiercely like Garuda of variegated plumage swooping down upon a snake. And both of them were foremost of bowmen, and both were endued with great strength, and both were capable of slaying foes. And seeing that an encounter was imminent between them, the Kauravas, anxious to witness it, stood aloof as lookers on. And beholding the offender Karna, the son of Pandu, excited to fury, and glad also at having him, soon made him, his horses, his car, and car-driver invisible by means of a frightful shower of countless arrows. And the warriors of the Bharatas headed by Bhishma, with their horses, elephants, and cars, pierced by Kiritin and rendered invisible by means of his shafts, their ranks also scattered and broken, began to wail aloud in grief. The illustrious and heroic Karna, however counteracting with numberless arrows of his own those shafts by Arjuna's hand, soon burst forth in view with bow and arrows like a blazing fire. And then there arose the sound of loud clapping of hands, with the blare of conchs and trumpets and kettle-drums made by the Kurus while they applauded Vikartana's son who filled the atmosphere with the sound of his bow-string flapping against his fence. And beholding Kiritin filling the air with the twang of *Gandiva*, and the upraised tail of the monkey that constituted his flag and that terrible creature yelling furiously from the top of his flagstaff, Karna sent forth a loud roar. And afflicting by means of his shafts, Vikartana's son along with his steeds, car and car-driver, Kiritin impetuously poured an arrowy shower on him, casting his eyes on the grandsire and Drona and Kripa. And Vikartana's son also poured upon Partha a heavy shower of arrows like a rain-charged cloud. And the diadem-decked Arjuna also covered Karna with a thick down-pour of keen-edged shafts. And the two heroes stationed on their cars, creating clouds of keen-edged arrows in a combat carried on by means of countless shafts and weapons, appeared to the spectators like the sun and the moon covered by clouds, and the light-handed Karna, unable to bear the sight of the foe, pierced the four horses of the diadem-decked hero with whetted arrows, and then struck his car-driver with three shafts, and his flagstaff also with three. Thus struck, that grinder of all adversaries in battle, that bull of the Kuru race, Jishnu wielding the *Gandiva,* like a lion awaked from slumber, furiously attacked Karna by means of straight-going arrows. And afflicted by the arrowy shower (of Karna), that illustrious achiever of super-human deeds soon displayed a thick shower of arrows in return. And he covered Karna's car with countless shafts like the sun covering the different worlds with rays. And like a lion attacked by an elephant, Arjuna, taking some keen crescent-shaped arrows from out of his quiver and drawing his bow to his ear, pierced the *Suta's* son on every part of his body. And that grinder of foes pierced Karna's arms and thighs and head and forehead and neck and other principal parts of his body with whetted shafts endued with the impetuosity of the thunderbolt and shot from the *Gandiva* in battle. And mangled and afflicted by the arrows shot by Partha the son of Pandu, Vikartana's son, quitted the van of battle, and quickly took to flight, like one elephant vanquished by another.'"

SECTION LV

Vaisampayana said, "After the son of Radha had fled from the field, other warriors headed by Duryodhana, one after another, fell upon the son of Pandu with their respective divisions. And like the shore withstanding the fury of the surging sea, that warrior withstood the rage of that countless host rushing towards him, arrayed in order of battle and showering clouds of arrows. And that foremost of car-warriors, Kunti's son Vibhatsu of white steeds, rushed towards the foe, discharging celestial weapons all the while. Partha soon covered all the points of the horizon with countless arrows shot from the *Gandiva*, like the sun covering the whole earth with his rays. And amongst those that fought on cars and horses and elephants, and amongst the mail-clad foot-soldiers, there was none that had on his body a space of even two finger's breadth unwounded with sharp arrows. And for his dexterity in applying celestial weapons, and for the training of the steeds and the skill of Uttara, and for the coursing of his weapons, and his prowess and light-handedness, people began to regard Arjuna as the fire that blazeth forth during the time of the universal dissolution for consuming all created things. And none amongst the foe could cast his eyes on Arjuna who shone like a blazing fire of great effulgence. And mangled by the arrows of Arjuna, the hostile ranks looked like newly-risen clouds on the breast of a hill reflecting the solar rays, or like groves of *Asoka* trees resplendent with clusters of flowers. Indeed, afflicted by the arrows of Partha, the soldiers looked like these, or like a beautiful garland whose flowers gradually wither and drop away: And the all-pervading wind bore on its wings in the sky the torn flags and umbrellas of the hostile host. And affrighted at the havoc amongst their own ranks, the steeds fled in all directions, freed from their yokes by means of Partha's arrows and dragging after them broken portions of cars and elephants, struck on their ears and ribs and tusks and nether lips and other delicate parts of the body, began to drop down on the battle-field. And the earth, bestrewn in a short time with the corpses of elephants belonging to the Kauravas, looked like the sky overcast with masses of black clouds. And as that fire of blazing flames at the end of the *yuga* consumeth all perishable things of the world, both mobile and immobile, so did Partha, O king, consumeth all foes in battle. And by the energy of his weapons and the twang of his bow, and the preter-natural yells of the creatures stationed on his flagstaff, and the terrible roar of the monkey, and by the blast of his conch, that mighty grinder of foes, Vibhatsu, struck terror into the hearts of all the troops of Duryodhana. And the strength of every hostile warrior seemed, as it were, to be levelled to the dust at the very sight of Arjuna. And unwilling to commit the daring act of sin of slaying them that were defenceless, Arjuna suddenly fell back and attacked the army from behind by means of clouds of keen-edged arrows proceeding towards their aims like hawks let off by fowlers. And he soon covered the entire welkin with clusters of blood-drinking arrows. And as the (infinite) rays of the powerful sun, entering a small vessel, are contracted within it for want of space, so the countless shafts of Arjuna could not find space for their expansion even within the vast welkin. Foes were able to behold Arjuna's car, when near, only once, for immediately after, they were with their horses, sent to the other world. And as his arrows unobstructed by the bodies of foes always passed through them, so his car, unimpeded by hostile ranks, always passed through the latter. And, indeed, he began to toss about and agitate the hostile troops with great violence like the thousand-headed Vasuki sporting in the great ocean. And as Kiritin incessantly shot his shafts, the noise of the bow-string, transcending every sound, was so loud that the like of it had never been heard before by created beings. And the elephants crowding the field, their bodies pierced with (blazing) arrows with small intervals between looked like black clouds coruscated with solar rays. And ranging in all directions and shooting (arrows) right and left, Arjuna's bow was always to be seen drawn to a perfect circle. And the arrows of the wielder of the *Gandiva* never fell upon anything except the aim, even as the eye never dwelleth on anything that is not beautiful. And as the track of a herd of elephants marching through the forest is made of itself, so was the track was made of itself for the car of Kiritin. And struck and mangled by Partha, the hostile warriors thought that,—*Verily, Indra himself, desirous of Partha's victory, accompanied by all the immortals is slaying us*! And they also regarded Vijaya, who was making a terrible slaughter around, to be none else than Death himself who having assumed the form of Arjuna, was slaying all creatures. And the troops of the Kurus, struck by Partha, were so mangled and shattered that the scene looked like the achievement of Partha himself and could be compared with nothing else save what was observable in Partha's combats. And he severed the heads of foes, even as reapers cut off the tops of deciduous herbs. And the Kurus all lost their energy owing to the terror begot of Arjuna. And tossed and mangled by the Arjuna-gale, the forest of Arjuna's foes reddened the earth with purple secretions. And the dust mixed with blood, uplifted by the wind, made the very rays of the sun redder still. And soon the sun-decked sky became so red that it looked very much like the evening. Indeed, the sun ceaseth to shed his rays as soon as he sets, but the son of Pandu ceased not to shoot his shafts. And that hero of inconceivable energy overwhelmed, by means of all celestial weapons, all the great bowmen of the enemy, although they were possessed of great prowess. And Arjuna then shot three and seventy arrows of sharp points at Drona, and ten at Dussaha and eight at Drona's son, and twelve at Duhsasana, and three at Kripa, the son of Saradwat. And that slayer of foes pierced Bhishma, the son of Santanu, with arrows, and king Duryodhana with a hundred. And, lastly, he pierced Karna in the ear with a bearded shaft. And when that great bowmen Karna, skilled in all weapons, was thus pierced, and his horses and car and car-driver were all destroyed, the troops that supported him began to break. And beholding those soldiers break and give way the son of Virata desirous of knowing Partha's purpose, addressed him on the field of battle, and said, 'O Partha, standing on this beautiful car, with myself as charioteer, towards which division shall I go? For, commanded by thee, I would soon take thee thither.'

"Arjuna replied, 'O Uttara, yonder auspicious warrior whom thou seest cased in coat of tiger-skin and stationed on his car furnished with a blue-flag and drawn by red steeds, is Kripa. There is to be seen the van of Kripa's division. Take me thither. I shall show that great bowman my swift-handedness in archery. And that warrior whose flag beareth the device of an elegant water-pot worked in gold, is the preceptor Drona—that foremost of all wielders of weapons. He is always an object of regard with me, as also with all bearers of arms. Do thou, therefore, circumambulate that great hero cheerfully. Let us bend our heads there, for that is the eternal virtue. If Drona strikes my body first, then I shall strike him, for then he will not be able to resent it. There, close to Drona, that warrior whose flag beareth the device of a bow, is the preceptor's son, the great car-warrior Aswatthaman, who is always an object of regard with me as also with every bearer of arms. Do thou, therefore, stop again and again, while thou comest by his car. There, that warrior who stayeth on his car, cased in golden mail and surrounded by a third part of the army consisting of the most efficient troops, and whose flag beareth the device of an elephant in a ground of gold, is the illustrious king Duryodhana, the son of Dhritarashtra. O hero, take before him this thy car that is capable of grinding hostile cars. This king is difficult of being vanquished in battle and is capable of grinding all foes. He is regarded as the first of all Drona's disciples in lightness of hand. I shall, in battle, show him my superior swiftness in archery. There, that warrior whose flag beareth the device of a stout chord for binding elephants, is Karna, the son of Vikartana, already known to thee. When thou comest before that wicked son of Radha, be thou very careful, for he always challengeth me to an encounter. And that warrior whose flag is blue and beareth the device of five stars with a sun (in the centre), and who endued with great energy stayeth on his car holding a huge bow in hand and wearing excellent fences, and over whose head is an umbrella of pure white, who standeth at the head of a multitudinous array of cars with various flags and banners like the sun in advance of masses of black clouds, and whose mail of gold looks bright as the sun or the moon, and who with his helmet of gold striketh terror into my heart, is Bhishma, the son of Santanu and the grandsire of us all. Entertained with regal splendour by Duryodhana, he is very partial and well-affected towards that prince. Let him be approached last of all, for he may, even now, be an obstacle to me. While fighting with me, do thou carefully guide the steeds.' Thus addressed by him, Virata's son, O king, guided Savyasachin's car with great alacrity towards the spot where Kripa stood anxious to fight."

SECTION LVI

Vaisampayana said, "And the ranks of those fierce bowmen, the Kurus, looked like masses of clouds in the rainy season drifting before a gentle wind. And close (to those ranks of foot-soldiers) stood the enemy's horses ridden by terrible warriors. And there were also elephants of terrible mien, looking resplendent in beautiful armour, ridden by skilled combatants and urged on with iron crows and hooks. And, O king, mounted on a beautiful car, Sakra came there accompanied by the celestials,—the *Viswas* and *Maruts*. And crowded with gods, *Yakshas, Gandharvas* and *Nagas*, the firmament looked as resplendent as it does when bespangled with the planetary constellation in a cloudless night. And the celestials came there, each on his own car, desirous of beholding the efficacy of their weapons in human warfare, and for witnessing also the fierce and mighty combat that would take place when Bhishma and Arjuna would meet. And embellished with gems of every kind and capable of going everywhere at the will of the rider, the heavenly car of the lord of the celestials, whose roof was upheld by a hundred thousand pillars of gold with (a central) one made entirely of jewels and gems, was conspicuous in the clear sky. And there appeared on the scene three and thirty gods with Vasava (at their head)—and (many) *Gandharvas* and *Rakshasas* and *Nagas* and *Pitris*, together with the great *Rishis*. And seated on the car of the lord of the celestials, appeared the effulgent persons of kings, Vasumanas and Valakshas and Supratarddana, and Ashtaka and Sivi and Yayati and Nahusha and Gaya and Manu and Puru and Raghu and Bhanu and Krisaswa and Sagara and Nala. And there shone in a splendid array, each in its proper place the cars of Agni and Isa and Soma and Varuna and Prajapati and Dhatri and Vidhatri and Kuvera and Yama, and Alamvusha and Ugrasena and others, and of the *Gandharva* Tumburu. And all the celestials and the *Siddhas*, and all the foremost of sages came there to behold that encounter between Arjuna and the Kurus. And the sacred fragrance of celestial garlands filled the air like that of blossoming woods at the advent of spring. And the red and reddish umbrellas and robes and garlands and *chamaras* of the gods, as they were stationed there, looked exceedingly beautiful. And the dust of the earth soon disappeared and (celestial) effulgence lit up everything. And redolent of divine perfumes, the breeze began to soothe the combatants. And the firmament seemed ablaze and exceedingly beautiful, decked with already arrived and arriving cars of handsome and various make, all illumined with diverse sorts of jewels, and brought thither by the foremost of the celestials. And surrounded by the celestials, and wearing a garland of lotuses and lilies the powerful wielder of the thunderbolt looked exceedingly beautiful on his car. And the slayer of Vala, although he steadfastly gazed at his son on the field of battle, was not satiated with such gazing."

SECTION LVII

Vaisampayana said, "Beholding the army of the Kurus arrayed in order of battle, that descendant of the Kuru race, Partha, addressing Virata's son, said, 'Do thou proceed to the spot where Kripa, the son of Saradwat, is going by the southern side of that car whose flag is seen to bear the device of a golden altar.'"

Vaisampayana continued, "Hearing these words of Dhananjaya, the son of Virata urged, without a moment's delay, those steeds of silvery hue decked in golden armour. And making them adopt, one after another, every kind of the swifter paces, he urged those fiery steeds resembling the moon in colour. And versed in horse-lore, Uttara, having approached the Kuru host, turned back those steeds endued with the speed of the wind. And skilled in guiding vehicles, the prince of Matsya, sometimes wheeling about, and sometimes proceeding in circular mazes, and sometimes turning to the left, began to be wilder than the Kurus. And wheeling round, the intrepid and mighty son of Virata at last approached the car of Kripa, and stood confronting him. Then announcing his own name, Arjuna powerfully blew that best of conchs called *Devadatta,* of loud blare. And blown on the field of battle by the mighty Jishnu, the blare of that conch was heard like the splitting of a mountain. And seeing that the conch did not break into a hundred fragments when blown by Arjuna, the Kurus with all their warriors began to applaud it highly. And having reached the very heavens, that sound coming back was heard even like the crash of the thunderbolt hurled by Maghavat on the mountain breast. Thereupon that heroic and intrepid and mighty car-warrior, Saradwat's son Kripa, endued with strength and prowess, waxing wroth at Arjuna, and unable to bear that sound and eager for fight, took up his own sea-begotten conch and blew it vehemently. And filling the three worlds with that sound, that foremost of car-warriors took up a large bow and twanged the bow-string powerfully. And those mighty car-warriors equal unto two suns, standing opposed to each other, shone like two masses of autumnal clouds. Then Saradwat's son quickly pierced Partha, that slayer of hostile heroes, with ten swift and whetted arrows capable of entering into the very vitals. And Pritha's son also, on his part, drawing that foremost of weapons, the *Gandiva,* celebrated over the world, shot innumerable iron arrows, all capable of penetrating into the very core of the body. Thereupon Kripa, by means of whetted shafts, cut into hundreds and thousands of fragments, those blood-drinking arrows of Partha before they could come up. Then that mighty car-warrior, Partha also, in wrath displaying various manoeuvres, covered all sides with a shower of arrows. And covering the entire welkin with his shafts, that mighty warrior of immeasurable soul, the son of Pritha, enveloped Kripa with hundreds of shafts. And sorely afflicted by those whetted arrows resembling flames of fire, Kripa waxed wroth and quickly afflicting the high-souled Partha of immeasurable prowess with ten thousand shafts, set up on the field of battle a loud roar. Then the heroic Arjuna quickly pierced the four steeds of his adversary with four fatal arrows shot from the *Gandiva*, sharp and straight, and furnished with golden wings. And pierced by means of those whetted arrows resembling flames of fire those steeds suddenly reared themselves, and in consequence Kripa reeled off his place. And seeing Gautama thrown off his place, the slayer of hostile heroes, the descendant of the Kuru race, out of regard for his opponent's dignity, ceased to discharge his shafts at him. Then regaining his proper place, Gautama quickly pierced Savyasachin with ten arrows furnished with feathers of the *Kanka* bird. Then with a crescent-shaped arrow of keen edge, Partha cut off Kripa's bow and leathern fences. And soon Partha cut off Kripa's coat of mail also by means of arrows capable of penetrating the very vitals, but he did not wound his person. And divested of his coat of mail, his body resembled that of a serpent which hath in season cast off its slough. And as soon as his bow had been cut off by Partha, Gautama took up another and stringed it in a trice. And strange to say, that bow of him was also cut off by Kunti's son, by means of straight shafts. And in this way that slayer of hostile heroes, the son of Pandu, cut off other bows as soon as they were taken up, one after another, by Saradwat's son. And when all his bows were thus cut off, that mighty hero hurled, from his car, at Pandu's son, a javelin like unto the blazing thunderbolt. Thereupon, as the gold-decked javelin came whizzing through the air with the flash of a meteor, Arjuna cut it off by means of ten arrows. And beholding his dart thus cut off by the intelligent Arjuna, Kripa quickly took up another bow and almost simultaneously shot a number of crescent-shaped arrows. Partha, however, quickly cut them into fragments by means of ten keen-edged shafts, and endued with great energy, the son of Pritha then, inflamed with wrath on the field of battle, discharged three and ten arrows whetted on stone and resembling flames of fire. And with one of these he cut off the yoke of his adversary's car, and with four pierced his four steeds, and with the sixth he severed the head of his antagonist's car-driver from off his body. And with three that mighty car-warrior pierced, in that encounter, the triple bamboo-pole of Kripa's car and with two, its wheels. And with the twelfth arrow he cut off Kripa's flagstaff. And with the thirteenth Phalguna, who was like Indra himself as if smiling in derision, pierced Kripa in the breast. Then with his bow cut off, his car broken, his steeds slain, his car-driver killed, Kripa leapt down and taking up a mace quickly hurled it at Arjuna. But that heavy and polished mace hurled by Kripa was sent back along its course, struck by means of Arjuna's arrows. And then the warriors (of Kripa's division), desirous of rescuing the wrathful son of Saradwat encountered Partha from all sides and covered him with their arrows. Then the son of Virata, turning the steed to the left began to perform circuitous evolution called *Yamaka* and thus withstood all those warriors. And those illustrious bulls among men, taking Kripa with them who had been deprived of his car, led him away from the vicinity of Dhananjaya, the son of Kunti."

SECTION LVIII

Vaisampayana said, "After Kripa had thus been taken away, the invincible Drona of red steeds, taking up his bow to which he had already stringed an arrow, rushed towards Arjuna of white steeds. And beholding at no great distance from him the preceptor advancing on his golden car, Arjuna that foremost of victorious warriors, addressing Uttara, said, 'Blessed be thou, O friend, carry me before that warrior on whose high banner-top is seen a golden altar resembling a long flame of fire and decked with numerous flags placed around, and whose car is drawn by steeds that are red and large, exceedingly handsome and highly-trained, of face pleasant and of quiet mien, and like unto corals in colour and with faces of coppery hue, for that warrior is Drona with whom I desire to fight. Of long arms and endued with mighty energy possessed of strength and beauty of person, celebrated over all the worlds for his prowess, resembling Usanas himself in intelligence and Vrihaspati in knowledge of morality, he is conversant with the four *Vedas* and devoted to the practice of *Brahmacharya* virtues. O friend, the use of the celestial weapons together with the mysteries of their withdrawal and the entire science of weapons, always reside in him. Forgiveness, self-control, truth, abstention from injury, rectitude of conduct,—these and countless other virtues always dwell in that regenerate one. I desire to fight with that highly-blessed one on the field. Therefore, take me before the preceptor and carry me thither, O Uttara.'"

Vaisampayana continued, "Thus addressed by Arjuna, Virata's son urged his steeds decked with gold towards the car of Bharadwaja's son. And Drona also rushed towards the impetuously advancing Partha, the son of Pandu,—that foremost of car-warriors,—like an infuriate elephant rushing towards an infuriate compeer. And the son of Bharadwaja then blew his conch whose blare resembled that of a hundred trumpets. And at that sound the whole army become agitated like the sea in a tempest. And beholding those excellent steeds red in hue mingling in battle with Arjuna's steeds of swan-like whiteness endued with the speed of the mind, all the spectators were filled with wonder. And seeing on the field of battle those car-warriors—the preceptor Drona and his disciple Partha—both endued with prowess, both invincible, both well-trained, both possessed of great energy and great strength, engaged with each other, that mighty host of the Bharatas began to tremble frequently. And that mighty car-warrior Partha, possessed of great prowess and filled with joy upon reaching Drona's car on his own, saluted the preceptor. And that slayer of hostile heroes, the mighty armed son of Kunti, then addressed Drona in an humble and sweet tone, saying, 'Having completed our exile in the woods, we are now desirous of avenging our wrongs. Even invincible in battle, it doth not behove thee to be angry with us. O sinless one, I will not strike thee unless thou strikest me first. Even this is my intention. It behoveth thee to act as thou choosest.' Thus addressed Drona discharged at him more than twenty arrows. But the light-handed Partha cut them off before they could reach him. And at this, the mighty Drona, displaying his lightness of hand in the use of weapons, covered Partha's car with a thousand arrows. And desirous of angering, Partha, that hero of immeasurable soul, then covered his steeds of silvery whiteness with arrows whetted on stone and winged with the feathers of the *Kanka* bird. And when the battle between Drona and Kiritin thus commenced, both of them discharging in the encounter arrows of blazing splendour, both well-known for their achievements, both equal to the wind itself in speed, both conversant with celestial weapons, and both endued with mighty energy, began shooting clouds of arrows to bewilder the royal Kshatriyas. And all the warriors that were assembled there were filled with wonder at sight of all this. And they all admired Drona who quickly shot clouds of arrows exclaiming,—*Well done! Well done*! Indeed, *who else save Phalguna, is worthy of fighting with Drona in battle? Surely the duties of a Kshatriya are stern, for Arjuna fighteth with even his own preceptor*!—And it was thus that they who stood on the field of battle said unto one another. And inflamed with fire, those mighty-armed heroes standing before other, and each incapable of overcoming the other, covered each other with arrowy showers. And Bharadwaja's son, waxing wroth, drew his large and unconquerable bow plated on the back with gold, and pierced Phalguna with his arrows. And discharging at Arjuna's car innumerable whetted arrows possessed of solar effulgence, he entirely shrouded the light of the sun. And that great car-warrior of mighty arms, violently pierced Pritha's son with keen-edged shafts even as the clouds shower upon a mountain. Then taking up that foremost of bows, the *Gandiva,* destructive of foes and capable of withstanding the greatest strain, the impetuous son of Pandu cheerfully discharged countless shafts of various kinds adorned with gold, and that powerful warrior also baffled in a moment Drona's arrowy shower by means of those shafts shot from his own bow. And at this the spectators wondered greatly. And the handsome Dhananjaya, the son of Pritha, ranging on his car, displayed his weapons on all sides at the same time. And the entire welkin covered with his arrows, became one wide expanse of shade. And at this Drona become invisible like the sun enveloped in mist. And shrouded by those excellent arrows on all sides, Drona looked like a mountain on fire. And beholding his own car completely enveloped by the arrows of Pritha's son, Drona that ornament of battle, bent his terrible and foremost of bows whose noise was as loud as that of the clouds. And drawing that first of weapons, which was like unto a circle of fire, he discharged a cloud of keen-edged shafts. And then there were heard on the field loud sounds like the splitting of bamboos set on fire. And that warrior of immeasurable soul, shooting from his bow arrows furnished with golden wings, covered all sides, shrouding the very light of the sun. And those arrows with knots well-peeled off, and furnished with golden wings, looked like flocks of birds in the sky. And the arrows discharged by Drona from his bow, touching one another at the wings, appeared like one endless line in the sky. And those heroes, thus discharging their arrows decked with gold, seemed to cover the sky with showers of meteors. And furnished with feathers of the *Kanka* bird, those arrows looked like rows of cranes ranging in the autumnal sky. And the fierce and terrible encounter that took place between the illustrious Drona and Arjuna resembled that between Virata and Vasava of old. And discharging arrows at each other from bows drawn at their fullest stretch, they resembled two elephants assailing each other with their tusks. And those wrathful warriors—those ornaments of battle—fighting strictly according to established usage, displayed in that conflict various celestial weapons in due order. Then that foremost of victorious men, Arjuna, by means of his keen shafts resisted the whetted arrows shot by that best of preceptors. And displaying before the spectators various weapons, that hero of terrible prowess covered the sky with various kinds of arrows. And beholding that tiger among men, Arjuna, endued with fierce energy and intent upon striking him, that foremost of warriors and best of preceptors (from affection) began to fight with him playfully by means of smooth and straight arrows. And Bharadwaja's son fought on with Phalguna, resisting with his own the celestial weapons shot by the former. And the fight that took place between those enraged lions among men, incapable of bearing each other, was like unto encounter between the gods and the *Danavas*. And the son of Pandu repeatedly baffled with his own, the *Aindra*, the *Vayavya*, and the *Agneya* weapons that were shot by Drona. And discharging keen shafts, those mighty bowmen, by their arrowy showers completely covered the sky and made a wide expanse of shade. And then the arrows shot by Arjuna, falling on the bodies of hostile warriors, produced the crash of thunderbolt. O king, elephants, cars, and horses, bathed in blood, looked like *Kinsuka* trees crowned with flowers. And in that encounter between Drona and Arjuna, beholding the field covered with arms decked with bangles, and gorgeously-attired car-warriors, and coats of mail variegated with gold, and with banners lying scattered all about, and with warriors slain by means of Partha's arrows, the Kuru host became panic-stricken. And shaking their bows capable of bearing much strain, those combatants began to shroud and weaken each other with their shafts. And, O bull of the Bharata race, the encounter that took place between Drona and Kunti's son was dreadful in the extreme and resembled that between Vali and Vasava. And staking their very lives, they began to pierce each other straight arrows shot from their fully-stretched bow-strings. And a voice was heard in the sky applauding Drona, and saying, 'Difficult is the feat performed by Drona, inasmuch as he fighteth with Arjuna,—that grinder of foes, that warrior endued with mighty energy, of firm grasp, and invincible in battle,—that conqueror of both celestials and *Daityas*, that foremost of all car-warriors.' And beholding Partha's infallibility, training, fleetness of hand, and the range also of Arjuna's, arrows, Drona became amazed. And, O bull of the Bharata race, lifting up his excellent bow, the *Gandiva*, the unforbearing Partha drew it now with one hand and now with another shot an arrowy shower. And beholding that shower resembling a flight of locusts, the spectators wondering applauded him exclaiming, 'Excellent! Excellent!' And so ceaselessly did he shoot his arrows that the very air was unable to penetrate the thick array. And the spectators could not perceive any interval between the taking up of the arrows and letting them off. And in that fierce encounter characterised by lightness of hand in the discharge of weapons, Partha began to shoot his arrows more quickly than before. And then all at once hundreds and thousands of straight arrows fell upon Drona's car. And, O bull of the Bharata race, beholding Drona completely covered by the wielder of the *Gandiva* with his arrows, the Kuru army set up exclamation of *'Oh'!* and *'Alas'!* And Maghavat, together with those *Gandharvas* and *Apsaras* that have come there, applauded the fleetness of Partha's hand. And that mighty car-warrior, the preceptor's son, then resisted the Pandva with a mighty array of cars. And although enraged with Arjuna, yet Aswatthaman mentally admired that feat of the high-souled son of Pritha. And waxing wroth, he rushed towards Partha, and discharged at him an arrowy shower like a heavy down-pour by the cloud. And turning his steeds towards Drona's son, Partha gave Drona an opportunity to leave the field. And thereupon the latter, wounded in that terrible encounter, and his mail and banner gone sped away by the aid of swift horses."

SECTION LIX

Vaisampayana said, "Then, O mighty king, Drona's son rushed to an encounter with Arjuna in battle. And beholding his rush to the conflict like a hurricane, showering shafts like a rain charged cloud Pritha's son received him with a cloud of arrows. And terrible was the encounter between them, like that between the gods and the *Danavas*. And they shot arrows at each other like Virata and Vasava. And the welkin being enveloped on all sides with arrows, the sun was completely hidden, and the air itself was hushed. And, O conqueror of hostile cities, as they assailed and struck each other, loud sounds arose as of bamboos on fire. And, O king, Aswatthaman's horses being sorely afflicted by Arjuna, they became bewildered and could not ascertain which way to go. And as Pritha's son ranged on the field, the powerful son of Drona finding an opportunity, cut off the string of the *Gandiva* with an arrow furnished with a horse-shoe head. And beholding that extraordinary feat of his, the celestials applauded him highly. And exclaiming—'Well done!'—'Well done!' Drona and Bhishma, and Karna, and the mighty warrior Kripa, all applauded that feat of his greatly. And the son of Drona, drawing his excellent bow, pierced with his shafts, furnished with the feathers of the *Kanka* bird, the breast of Partha, that bull among warriors. Thereupon, with a loud laughter, the mighty-armed son of Pritha attached a strong and fresh string to *Gandiva*. And moistening his bow-string with the sweat that stood on his forehead resembling the crescent moon, Pritha's son advanced towards his adversary, even as an infuriated leader of a herd of elephants rusheth at another elephant. And the encounter that took place between those two matchless heroes on the field of battle was exceedingly fierce and made the bristles of the spectators stand on their ends. And as those heroes endued with mighty energy fought on, the two mighty elephants, the Kurus beheld them with wonder. And those brave bulls among men assailed each other with arrows of snaky forms and resembling blazing fires. And as the couple of quivers belonging to the Pandava was inexhaustible, that hero was able to remain on the field immovable as a mountain. And as Aswatthaman's arrows, in consequence of his ceaseless discharge in that conflict, were quickly exhausted, it was for this that Arjuna prevailed over his adversary. Then Karna, drawing his large bow with great force twanged the bow-string. And thereupon arose loud exclamation of *'Oh!'* and *'Alas!'* And Pritha's son, casting his eyes towards the spot where that bow was twanged, beheld before him the son of Radha. And at that sight his wrath was greatly excited. And inflamed with ire and desirous of slaying Karna, that bull of the Kuru race stared at him with rolling eyes. And, O king, beholding Partha turn away from Aswatthaman's side, the Kuru warriors discharged thousands of arrows on Arjuna. And the mighty-armed Dhananjaya, that conqueror of foes, leaving Drona's son, all on a sudden rushed towards Karna. And rushing towards Karna, with eyes reddened in anger the son of Kunti, desirous of a single combat with him, said these words."

SECTION LX

"Arjuna said, 'The time, O Karna, hath now come for making good thy loquacious boast in the midst of the assembly, viz., that there is none equal to thee in fight. Today, O Karna, contending with me in terrible conflict, thou shalt know thy own strength, and shalt no longer disregard others. Abandoning good breeding, thou hadst uttered many harsh words, but this that thou endeavourest to do, is, I think, exceedingly difficult. Do thou now, O Radha's son, contending with me in the sight of the Kurus, make good what thou hadst said before in disregard of myself. Thou who hadst witnessed Panchala's princess outraged by villains in the midst of the court, do thou now reap the fruit of that act of thine. Fettered by the bonds of morality before, I desisted from vengeance then. Behold now, O son of Radha, the fruit of that wrath in conflict at hand. O wicked wight, we have suffered much misery in that forest for full twelve years. Reap thou today the fruits of our concentrated vengeance. Come, O Karna, cope with me in battle. Let these thy Kaurava warriors witness the conflict.' Hearing these words, Karna replied, 'Do thou, O Partha, accomplish in deed what thou sayst in words. The world knows that thy words verily exceed thy deed. That thou hadst foreborne formerly was owing to thy inability to do anything. If we witness thy prowess even now, we may acknowledge its truth. If thy past forbearance was due to thy having been bound by the bonds of morality, truly thou art equally bound now although thou regardest thyself free. Having as thou sayst, passed thy exile in the woods in strict accordance with thy pledge and being therefore weakened by practising an ascetic course of life, how canst thou desire a combat with me now! O Pritha's son, if Sakra himself fight on thy side, still I would feel no anxiety in putting forth my prowess. Thy wish, O son of Kunti, is about to be gratified. Do thou fight with me now, and behold my strength.' Hearing this, Arjuna said, 'Even now, O Radha's son, thou hadst fled from battle with me, and it is for this that thou livest although thy younger brother hath been slain. What other person, save thee, having beheld his younger brother slain in battle would himself fly from the field, and boast as thou dost, amid good and true men?'"

Vaisampayana continued, "Having said these words unto Karna, the invincible Vibhatsu rushed at him and charged a volley of shafts capable of penetrating through a coat of mail. But that mighty car-warrior, Karna, received with great alacrity that discharge with an arrowy shower of his own, heavy as the downpour of the clouds. And that fierce volley of arrows covered all sides and severally pierced the steeds and arms and leathern fences of the combatants. And incapable of putting up with that assault, Arjuna cut off the strings of Karna's quiver by means of a straight and sharp arrow. Thereupon, taking out from his quiver another arrow, Karna pierced the Pandava in the hand at which the latter's hold of the bow was loosened. And then the mighty-armed Partha cut off Karna's bow into fragments. And Karna replied by hurling a dart at his adversary, but Arjuna cut it off by means of his arrows. And then the warriors that followed the son of Radha rushed in crowds at Arjuna, but Partha sent them all to the abode of Yama by means of arrows shot from the *Gandiva*. And Vibhatsu slew the steeds of Karna by means of sharp and tough arrows shot from the bow-string drawn to the ear, and deprived of life they dropped down on the ground. And taking another sharp and blazing arrow endued with great energy, the mighty son of Kunti pierced the breast of Karna. And that arrow, cleaving through his mail, penetrated into his body. And at this, Karna's vision was obscured and his senses left him. And regaining consciousness, he felt a great pain, and leaving the combat fled in a northernly direction. And at this, the mighty car-warrior Arjuna and Uttara, both began to address him contumely."

SECTION LXI

Vaisampayana said, "Having defeated Vikartana's son, Arjuna said unto the son of Virata, 'Take me towards that division where yonder device of a golden palmyra is seen. There our grandfather, Santanu's son, like unto a celestial, waiteth, desirous of an encounter with me.' Thereupon, beholding that mighty host thronged with cars and horses and elephants, Uttara, sorely pierced with arrows, said, 'O hero, I am no longer able to guide thy excellent steeds. My spirits droop and my mind is exceedingly bewildered. All the directions seem to be whirling before my eyes in consequence of the energy of the celestial weapons used by thee and the Kurus. I have been deprived of my senses by the stench of fat and blood and flesh. Beholding all this, from terror my mind is, as it were, cleft in twain. Never before had I beheld such a muster of horses in battle. And at the flapping of fences, and the blare of conchs, the leonine roars made by the warriors and the shrieks of elephants, and the twang of the *Gandiva* resembling the thunder, I have, O hero, been so stupefied that I have been deprived of both hearing and memory. And, O hero, beholding thee incessantly drawing to a circle, in course of the conflict, the *Gandiva* which resembleth a circle of fire, my sight faileth me and my heart is rent asunder. And seeing thy fierce form in battle, like that of the wielder of the *Pinaka* while inflamed with wrath, and looking also at the terrible arrows shot by thee, I am filled with fear. I fail to see when thou takest up thy excellent arrows, when thou fixest them on the bow-string, and when thou lettest them off. And though all this is done before my eyes, yet, deprived of my senses, I do not see it. My spirits are drooping and earth itself seems to be swimming before me. I have no strength to hold the whip and the reins.' Hearing these words, Arjuna said, 'Do thou not fear. Assure thyself. Thou also hast, on the field of battle performed, O bull among men, wonderful feats. Blessed be thou, thou art a prince and born in the illustrious line of Matsyas. It behoveth thee not to feel dispirited in chastising thy foes. Therefore, O prince, stationed on my car, muster all thy fortitude and hold the reins of my steeds, O slayer of foes, when I once more become engaged in battle.'"

Vaisampayana continued, "Having said this unto Virata's son, that best of men and foremost of car-warriors, the mighty-armed Arjuna, again addressed the son of Virata, saying. 'Take me without delay to the van of Bhishma's division. I will cut off his very bow-string in the battle. Thou shalt behold today the celestial weapons of blazing beauty, shot by me, look like flashes of lightning disporting amid the clouds in the sky. The Kauravas shall behold the gold decked back of my *Gandiva* today, and assembled together the foe shall dispute, saying,—*By which hand of his, the right or the left, doth he shoot*? And I shall cause a dreadful river (of death) to flow today towards the other world with blood for its waters and cars for its eddies, and elephants for its crocodiles. I shall today, with my straight arrows, extirpate the *Kuru* forest having hands and feet and heads and backs and arms for the branches of its trees. Alone, bow in hand, vanquishing the Kuru host, a hundred paths shall open before me like those of a forest in conflagration. Struck by me thou shalt today behold the Kuru army moving round and round like a wheel (unable to fly off the field). I shall show thee today my excellent training in arrows and weapons. Stay thou on my car firmly, whether the ground be smooth or uneven. I can pierce with my winged arrows even the mountain of *Sumeru* that stands touching the very heavens. I slew of old, at Indra's command, hundreds and thousands of *Paulomas* and *Kalakhanjas* in battle. I have obtained my firmness of grasp from Indra, and my lightness of hand from *Brahman*, and I have learnt various modes of fierce attack and defence amid crowds of foes from *Prajapati*. I vanquished, on the other side of the great ocean, sixty thousands of car-warriors—all fierce archers—residing in *Hiranyapura*. Behold, now I defeat the multitudinous host of the Kurus like a tempest scattering a heap of cotton. With my fiery arrows I shall today set the *Kuru*-forest to fire, having banners for its trees, the foot-soldiers for its shrubs, and the car-warriors for its beasts of prey. Like unto the wielder of the thunderbolt overthrowing the Danavas, alone I shall, with my straight arrows, bring down from the chambers of their cars the mighty warrior of the Kuru army stationed therein and struggling in the conflict to the best of their power. I have obtained from *Rudra* the *Raudra*, from *Varuna* the *Varuna*, from *Agni* the *Agneya*, from the god of Wind the *Vayava*, and from Sakra the thunderbolt and other weapons. I shall certainly exterminate the fierce *Dhartarashtra-forest* though protected by many leonine warriors. Therefore, O Virata's son, let thy fears be dispelled.'"

Vaisampayana continued, "Thus assured by Savyasachin, the son of Virata penetrated into that fierce array of cars protected by Bhishma. The son of Ganga, however, of fierce deeds, cheerfully withstood the mighty-armed hero advancing from desire of vanquishing the heroes in battle. Jishnu, then, confronting Bhishma, cut off his standard clean off at the roots by shooting a gold-decked arrow pierced by which it fell to the ground. And at this, four mighty warriors, Duhsasana and Vikarna and Dussaha and Vivingsati, skilled in weapons and endued with great energy, and all decked with handsome garlands and ornaments, rushed towards that terrible bowman. And advancing towards Vibhatsu—that fierce archer, these all encompassed him around. Then the heroic Duhsasana pierced the son of Virata with a crescent-shaped arrow and he pierced Arjuna with another arrow in the breast. And Jishnu, confronting Duhsasana, cut off by means of a sharp-edged arrow furnished with vulturine wings his adversary's bow plaited with gold, and then pierced his person in the breast by means of five arrows. And afflicted by the arrows of Partha, Duhsasana fled, leaving the combat. Then Vikarna, the son of Dhritarashtra, pierced Arjuna—that slayer of hostile heroes, by means of sharp and straight arrows furnished with vulturine wings. But the son of Kunti within a moment hit him also in the forehead with straight shafts. And pierced by Arjuna, he fell down from his car. And at this, Dussaha, supported by Vivingsati, covered Arjuna with a cloud of sharp arrows, impelled by the desire of rescuing his brother. Dhananjaya, however, without the least anxiety, pierced both of them almost at the same instant by means of couple of keen-edged arrows and then slew the steeds of both. And there upon, both those sons of Dhritarashtra, deprived of their steeds and their bodies mangled were taken away by the warrior behind them who had rushed forward with other cars. Then the unvanquished Vibhatsu, the mighty son of Kunti, decked with diadem and sure of aim, simultaneously attacked all sides with his arrows."

SECTION LXII

Vaisampayana said, "Then, O thou of the Bharata race, all the great car-warriors of the Kurus, united together, began to assail Arjuna to the best of their might from all sides. But that hero of immeasurable soul completely covered all those mighty car-warriors with clouds of arrows, even as the mist covereth the mountains. And the roars of huge elephants and conchs, mingling together, produced a loud up roar. And penetrating through the bodies of elephants and horses as also through steel coats of mail, the arrows shot by Partha fell by thousands. And shooting shafts with the utmost celerity, the son of Pandu seemed in that contest to resemble the blazing sun of an autumnal midday. And afflicted with fear, the car-warriors began to leap down from their cars and the horse-soldiers from horse-back, while the foot-soldiers began to fly in all directions. And loud was the clatter made by Arjuna's shafts as they cleft the coats of mail belonging to mighty warriors, made of steel, silver, and copper. And the field was soon covered with the corpses of warriors mounted on elephants and horses, all mangled by the shafts of Partha of great impetuosity like unto sighing snakes. And then it seemed as if Dhananjaya, bow in hand, was dancing on the field of battle. And sorely affrighted at the twang of the *Gandiva* resembling the noise of the thunder, many were the combatants that fled from that terrible conflict. And the field of battle was bestrewn with severed heads decked with turbans, ear-rings and necklaces of gold, and the earth looked beautiful by being scattered all over with human trunks mangled by shafts, and arms having bows in their grasp and hands decked with ornaments. And, O bull of the Bharata race, in consequence of heads cut off by whetted shafts ceaselessly falling on the ground, it seemed as if a shower of stones fell from the sky. And that Partha of formidable prowess, displaying his fierceness, now ranged the field of battle, pouring the terrible fire of his wrath upon the sons of Dhritarashtra. And beholding the fierce prowess of Arjuna who thus scorched the hostile host, the Kuru warriors, in the very presence of Duryodhana, became dispirited and ceased to fight. And, O Bharata, having struck terror into that host and routed those mighty car-warriors, that foremost of victors, ranged on the field. And the son of Pandu then created on the field of battle a dreadful river of blood, with waving billows, like unto the river of death that is created by Time at the end of the *Yuga*, having the dishevelled hair of the dead and the dying for its floating moss and straw, with bows and arrows for its boats, fierce in the extreme and having flesh and animal juices for its mire. And coats of mail and turbans floated thick on its surface. And elephants constituted its alligators and the cars its rafts. And marrow and fat and blood constituted its currents. And it was calculated to strike terror into the hearts of the spectators. And dreadful to behold, and fearful in the extreme, and resounding with the yells of ferocious beasts, keen edged weapons constituted its crocodiles. And *Rakshasas* and other cannibals haunted it from one end to the other. And strings of pearls constituted its ripples, and various excellent ornaments, its bubbles. And having swarms of arrows for its fierce eddies and steeds for its tortoises, it was incapable of being crossed. And the mighty car warrior constituted its large island, and it resounded with the blare of conchs and the sound of drums. And the river of blood that Partha created was incapable of being crossed. Indeed, so swift-handed was Arjuna that the spectators could not perceive any interval between his taking up an arrow, and fixing it on the bow-string, and letting it off by a stretch of the *Gandiva*."

SECTION LXIII

Vaisampayana said, "Then while a great havoc was being made among the Kurus, Santanu's son, Bhishma, and grandsire of the Bharatas rushed at Arjuna, taking up an excellent bow adorned with gold, and many arrows also of keen points and capable of piercing into the very vitals of the foe and afflicting him sorely. And in consequence of a white umbrella being held over his head, that tiger among men looked beautiful like unto a hill at sunrise. And the son of Ganga, blowing his conch cheered the sons of Dhritarashtra, and wheeling along his right came upon Vibhatsu and impeded his course. And that slayer of hostile heroes, the son of Kunti, beholding him approach, received him with a glad heart, like a hill receiving a rain-charged cloud. And Bhishma, endued with great energy, pierced Partha's flag-staff with eight arrows. The arrows reaching the flag-staff of Pandu's son, struck the blazing ape and those creatures also stationed in the banner-top. And then the son of Pandu, with a mighty javelin of sharp edge cut of Bhishma's umbrella which instantly fell on the ground. And then the light-handed son of Kunti struck his adversary's flag-staff also with many shafts, and then his steeds and then the couple of drivers that protected Bhishma's flanks. And unable to bear this, Bhishma though cognisant of the Pandava's might, covered Dhananjaya with a powerful celestial weapon. And the son of Pandu, of immeasurable soul, hurling in return a celestial weapon at Bhishma, received that from Bhishma like a hill receiving a deep mass of clouds. And the encounter that took place between Partha and Bhishma, was fierce and the Kaurava warriors with their troops stood as lookers on. And in the conflict between Bhishma and the son of Pandu, shafts striking against shafts shone in the air like fireflies in the season of rains. And, O king, in consequence of Partha's shooting arrows with both his right and left hands, the bent *Gandiva* seemed like a continuous circle of fire. And the son of Kunti then covered Bhishma with hundreds of sharp and keen-edged arrows, like a cloud covering the mountain-breast with its heavy downpour. And Bhishma baffled with his own arrows that arrowy shower, like the bank resisting the swelling sea, and covered the son of Pandu in return. And those warriors, cut into a thousand pieces in battle, fell fast in the vicinity of Phalguna's car. And then there was a downpour, from the car of Pandu's son, of arrows furnished with golden wing, and raining through the sky like a flight of locusts. And Bhishma again repelled that arrowy shower with hundreds of whetted shafts shot by him. And then the Kauravas exclaimed.—'Excellent! Excellent!—Indeed, Bhishma hath performed an exceedingly difficult feat inasmuch as he hath fought with Arjuna. Dhananjaya is mighty and youthful, and dexterous and swift of hand. Who else, save Bhishma, the son of Santanu, or Krishna, the son of Devaki, or the mighty son of Bharadwaja, the foremost of preceptors, is able to bear the impetus of Partha in battle?' And repelling weapons with weapons, those two bulls of the Bharata race, both endued with great might, fought on playfully and infatuated the eyes of all created beings. And those illustrious warriors ranged on the field of battle, using the celestials weapons obtained from *Prajapati* and *Indra*, and *Agni* and the fierce *Rudra*, and *Kuvera*, and *Varuna*, and *Yama*, and *Vayu*. And all beings were greatly surprised, upon beholding those warriors engaged in combat. And they all exclaimed,—*Bravo Partha of long arms! Bravo Bhishma! Indeed, this application of celestial weapons that is being witnessed in the combat between Bhishma and Partha* is rare among human beings."

Vaisampayana continued, "Thus raged that conflict with weapons between those warriors conversant with all weapons. And when that conflict of celestial weapons ceased, then commenced a conflict with arrows. And Jishnu approaching his opponent, cut off with an arrow sharp like a razor the gold-decked bow of Bhishma. Within the twinkling of the eye, however, Bhishma, that mighty-armed and great car-warrior, took up another bow and stringed it. And inflamed with wrath, he showered upon Dhananjaya a cloud of arrows. And Arjuna, too, endued with great energy, rained upon Bhishma innumerable sharp-pointed and keen-edged arrows. And Bhishma also shot clouds of arrows upon Pandu's son. And conversant with celestial weapons and engaged in shooting and each other, arrows of keen points, no distinction, O king, could then be perceived between those illustrious warriors. And that mighty car-warrior, Kunti's son, covered with a diadem, and the heroic son of Santanu, obscured the ten directions with their arrows. And the Pandava covered Bhishma, and Bhishma also covered the Pandava, with clouds of shafts. And, O king, wonderful was this combat that took place in this world of men. And the heroic warriors that protected Bhishma's car, slain by the son of Pandu, fell prostrate, O monarch, beside the car of Kunti's son. And the feathery arrows of Swetavahana, shot from the *Gandiva*, fell in all directions as if with the object of making a wholesale slaughter of the foe. And issuing forth from his car those blazing arrows furnished with golden wings looked like rows of swans in the sky. And all the celestials with Indra, stationed in the firmament, gazed with wonder upon another celestial weapon hurled with great force by that wonderful archer Arjuna. And beholding that wonderful weapon of great beauty, the mighty *Gandiva*, Chitrasena, highly pleased, addressed the lord of celestials, saying, 'Behold these arrows shot by Partha coursing through the sky in one continuous line. Wonderful is the dexterity of Jishnu in evolving this celestial weapon! Human beings are incapable of shooting such a weapon, for it does not exist among men. How wonderful again is this concourse of mighty weapons existing from days of old! No interval can be perceived between his taking up the arrows, fixing them on the bow-string, and letting them off by stretching the *Gandiva*. The soldiers are incapable of even looking at the son of Pandu, who is like unto the midday sun blazing in the sky. So also none ventures to look at Bhishma, the son of Ganga. Both are famous for their achievements, and both are of fierce prowess. Both are equal in feats of heroism, and both are difficult of being vanquished in battle.'

"Thus addressed by the *Gandharva* about that combat between Partha and Bhishma, the lord of the celestials, O Bharata, paid proper respect unto both by a shower of celestial flowers. Meanwhile, Bhishma, the son of Santanu, assailed Arjuna on the left side, while that drawer of the bow with either hands was on the point of piercing him. And at this, Vibhatsu, laughing aloud, cut off with an arrow of keen edge and furnished with vulturine wings, the bow of Bhishma, that hero of solar effulgence. And then Dhananjaya, the son of Kunti, pierced Bhishma in the breast with ten shafts although the latter was contending with all his prowess. And sorely afflicted with pain Ganga's son of mighty arms and irresistible in battle, stood for a long time leaning on the pole of his car. And beholding him deprived of consciousness the driver of his car-steeds, calling to mind the instructions about protecting the warriors when in a swoon, led him away for safety."

SECTION LXIV

Vaisampayana said, "After Bhishma had fled, leaving the van of battle, the illustrious son of Dhritarashtra hoisting high flag approached Arjuna, bow in hand and setting up a loud roar. And with a spear-headed shaft shot from his bow stretched to the ear, he pierced on the forehead of that terrible bowman of fierce prowess, Dhananjaya, ranging amidst the foes. And pierced with that keen shaft of golden point on the forehead, that hero of famous deeds looked resplendent, O king, like unto a beautiful hill with a single peak. And cut by that arrow, the warm life-blood gushed out profusely from the wound. And the blood trickling down his body shone beautifully like a wreath of golden flowers. And struck by Duryodhana with the shaft, the swift-handed Arjuna of unfailing strength, swelling with rage, pierced the king in return, taking up arrows that were endued with the energy of snakes of virulent poison. And Duryodhana of formidable energy attacked Partha, and Partha also, that foremost of heroes, attacked Duryodhana. And it was that those foremost of men, both born in the race of Ajamida, struck each other alike in the combat. And then (seated) on an infuriate elephant huge as a mountain and supported by four cars, Vikarna rushed against Jishnu, the son of Kunti. And beholding that huge elephant, advancing with speed, Dhananjaya struck him on the head between the temples with an iron arrow of great impetus shot from the bow-string stretched to the ear. And like the thunderbolt hurled by Indra splitting a mountain, that arrow furnished with vulturine wings, shot by Partha, penetrated, up to the very feathers, into the body of that elephant huge as hill. And sorely afflicted by the shaft, that lord of the elephant species began to tremble, and deprived of strength fell down on the ground in intense anguish, like the peak of mountain riven by thunder. And that best of elephants falling down on the earth, Vikarna suddenly alighting in great terror, ran back full eight hundred paces and ascended on the car of Vivingsati. And having slain with that thunder-like arrow that elephant huge as a mighty hill and looking like a mass of clouds, the son of Pritha smote Duryodhana in the breast with another arrow of the same kind. And both the elephant and the king having thus been wounded, and Vikarna having broken and fled along with the supporters of the king's car, the other warriors, smitten with the arrows shot from the *Gandiva*, fled from the field in panic. And beholding the elephant slain by Partha, and all the other warriors running away, Duryodhana, the foremost of the Kurus, turning away his car precipitately fled in that direction where Partha was not. And when Duryodhana was fast running away in alarm, pierced by that arrow and vomitting forth blood, Kiritin, still eager for battle and capable of enduring every enemy, thus censured him from wrath, 'Sacrificing thy great fame and glory, why dost thou fly away, turning thy back? Why are not those trumpets sounded now, as they were when thou hadst set out from thy kingdom? Lo, I am an obedient servant of Yudhishthira, myself being the third son of Pritha, standing here for battle. Turn back, show me thy face, O son of Dhritarashtra, and bear in thy mind the behaviour of kings. The name *Duryodhana* bestowed on thee before is hereby rendered meaningless. When thou runnest away, leaving the battle, where is thy persistence in battle? Neither do I behold thy body-guards, O Duryodhana, before nor behind. O foremost of men, fly thou away and save thy life which is dear from the hands of Pandu's son.'"

SECTION LXV

Vaisampayana said, "Thus summoned to battle by the illustrious hero, Dhritarashtra's son turned back stung by those censures, like an infuriate and mighty elephant pricked by a hook. And stung by those reproaches and unable to bear them, that mighty and brave car-warrior endued with great swiftness, turned back on his car, like a snake that is trampled under foot. And beholding Duryodhana turn back with his wounds, Karna, that hero among men, decked with a golden necklace, stopped the king on the way and soothing him, himself proceeded along the north of Duryodhana's car to meet Partha in battle. And the mighty-armed Bhishma also, the son of Santanu, turning back his steeds decked with gold, enormous in size, and of tawny hue, rushed bow in hand, for protecting Duryodhana from Partha's hand. And Drona and Kripa and Vivingsati and Duhsasana and others also, quickly turning back, rushed forward with speed with drawn bows and arrows fixed on the bow-strings, for protecting Duryodhana. And beholding those divisions advance towards him like the swelling surges of the ocean, Dhananjaya, the son of Pritha, quickly rushed at them like a crane rushing at a descending cloud. And with celestial weapons in their hands, they completely surrounded the son of Pritha and rained on him from all sides a perfect shower of shafts, like clouds showering on the mountain breast a heavy downpour of rain. And warding off with weapons, all the weapons of those bulls among the Kurus, the wielder of the *Gandiva* who was capable of enduring all foes, evolved another irresistible weapon obtained from Indra, called *Sanmohana*. And entirely covering the cardinal and other directions with sharp and keen-edged arrows furnished with beautiful feathers, that mighty hero stupefied their senses with the twang of the *Gandiva*. And once more, taking up with both his hands that large conch of loud blare, Partha, that slayer of foes, blew it with force and filled the cardinal and other points, the whole earth, and sky, with that noise. And those foremost of the Kuru heroes were all deprived of their senses by the sound of that conch blown by Partha. And all of them stood still, their bows, from which they were never separated, dropping down from their hands. And when the Kuru army became insensible, Partha calling to mind the words of Uttara, addressed the son of the Matsya king, saying, 'O best of men, go thou among the Kurus, so long as they remain insensible, and bring away the white garments of Drona and Kripa, and the yellow and handsome ones of Karna, as also the blue ones of the king and Drona's son. Methinks, Bhishma is not stupefied, for he knoweth how to counteract this weapon of mine. So, pass thou on, keeping his steeds to thy left; for those that are sensible should thus be avoided.' Hearing these words, the illustrious son of Matsya, giving up the reins of the steeds, jumped down from the car and taking off the garments of the warriors, came back to his place. And the son of Virata then urged the four handsome steeds with flanks adorned with golden armours. And those white steeds, urged on, took Arjuna away from the midst of battle-field and beyond the array of the infantry bearing standards in their hands. And, Bhishma, beholding that best of men thus going away, struck him with arrows. And Partha, too, having slain Bhishma's steeds, pierced him with ten shafts. And abandoning Bhishma on the field of battle, having first slain his car-driver, Arjuna with a good-looking bow in hand came out of that multitude of cars, like the sun emerging from the clouds. And Dhritarashtra's son, that foremost of heroes among the Kurus, recovering his senses, saw the son of Pritha standing like the lord of the celestials, alone on the battle-field. And he said in hurry (unto Bhishma), 'How hath this one escape from thee? Do thou afflict him in such a way that he may not escape.' And at this, Santanu's son, smiling, said unto him, 'Where had been this sense of thine, and where had been thy prowess too, when thou hadst been in a state of unconsciousness renouncing thy arrows and handsome bow? Vibhatsu is not addicted to the commission of atrocious deeds; nor is his soul inclined to sin. He renounceth not his principles even for the sake of the three worlds. It is for this only that all of us have not been slain in this battle. O thou foremost of Kuru heroes, go back to the city of the Kurus, and let Partha also go away, having conquered the kine. Do thou never foolishly throw away thy own good. Indeed, that which leadeth to one's welfare ought to be accomplished.'"

Vaisampayana continued, "Having listened to the words of the grandsire that tended to his own welfare, the wrathful king Duryodhana no longer eager for battle, drew a deep sigh and became silent. And reflecting that the advice of Bhishma was beneficial and seeing that the Pandavas gaining in strength, the other warriors also, desirous of protecting Duryodhana, resolved to return. And beholding those foremost of Kuru heroes departing for their city, Dhananjaya, the son of Pritha, with a cheerful heart followed them for a while, desirous of addressing and worshipping them. And having worshipped the aged grandsire—the son of Santanu, as also the preceptor Drona, and having saluted with beautiful arrows Drona's son and Kripa and other venerable ones among the Kurus, the son of Pritha broke into fragments Duryodhana's crown decked with precious gems, with another arrow. And having saluted all the venerable and brave warriors thus, he filled the three worlds with the twang of the *Gandiva*. And suddenly blowing his conch called *Devadatta*, the hero pierced the hearts of all his foes. And having humbled the hostile, he looked resplendent on his car decked with a handsome flag. And beholding the Kurus depart, Kiritin cheerfully said unto Matsya's son, 'Turn back thy steeds; thy kine have been recovered; the foe is going away and do thou also return to thy city with a cheerful heart.' And the celestials also, having witnessed that most wonderful encounter between Phalguna and the Kurus, were highly delighted, and went to their respective abodes, reflecting upon Partha's feats."

SECTION LXVI

Vaisampayana said, "Having vanquished the Kurus in battle, that one with eyes like those of a bull brought back that profuse cattle wealth of Virata. And while the Dhritarashtra, after their rout, were going away, a large number of Kuru-soldiers issuing out of the deep forest appeared with slow steps before Partha, their hearts afflicted with fear. And they stood before him with joined palms and with hair dishevelled. And fatigued with hunger and thirst, arrived in a foreign land, insensible with terror, and confused in mind, they all bowed down unto the son of Pritha and said,—*We are thy slaves.*'

"Arjuna said, 'Welcome, blessed be ye. Go ye away. Ye have no cause of fear. I will not take the lives of them that are afflicted. Ye have my assurance of protection.'"

Vaisampayana continued, "Hearing these words of assurance, the assembled warriors greeted him with benedictions in praise of his achievements and fame and wishing him long life. And the Kauravas were unable to confront Arjuna while after routing the foe he proceeded towards the city of Virata, like an elephant with rent temples. And having routed the whole army of the Kuru like a violent wind scattering the clouds, that slayer of foes, Partha, regardfully addressing the prince of Matsya, said, 'It is known to thee alone, O child, that the sons of Pritha are all living with thy father. Do not eulogise them upon entering the city, for then the king of the Matsyas may hide himself in fear. On the other hand, entering the city, do thou proclaim in the presence of thy father that the deed is thy own, saying,—*By me hath the army of the Kurus been vanquished and by me have the kine been recovered from the foe!*'

"Uttara said, 'The feat thou hast achieved is beyond my power. I do not possess the ability to achieve it. I shall not, however, O Savyasachin, discover thee to my father, as long as thou wilt not tell me to do it.'"

Vaisampayana continued, "Having vanquished the hostile army and wrested the whole of the cattle wealth from the Kurus, Jishnu returned again to the cemetery and having approached the same *Sami* tree stood there with body mangled by the arrows of the enemy. Then that terrible monkey blazing like fire ascended into the sky with those other creatures in the flag-staff. And the illusion created (by Viswakarma) melted away and Uttara's own banner bearing the device of a lion was set up on the car again. And having replaced the arrows and quivers of those foremost of the Kuru princes, and also that other weapon the *(Gandiva)* which enhances the fierceness of a battle, the illustrious prince of Matsya set out for the city with a glad heart, having Kiritin as his charioteer. And having achieved an exceedingly mighty feat and slain the foe, Partha also, that slayer of foes, binding his hair into a braid as before, took the reins from Uttara's hands. And that illustrious hero entered the city of Virata, with a cheerful heart rehabilitating himself as Vrihannala, the car-driver of Uttara.'"

Vaisampayana continued, "When all the Kauravas utterly routed and vanquished, set out in a dejected mood for Hastinapura, Phalguna, on his way back, addressed Uttara, saying, 'O prince, O hero of mighty arms, seeing the kine escorted in advance of us by the cowherds, we shall enter Virata's metropolis in the afternoon, having tended the steeds with drink and a bath. Let the cowherds, despatched by thee, speedily repair to the city with the good news and proclaim thy victory.'"

Vaisampayana continued, "Agreeable to Arjuna's words, Uttara speedily ordered the messengers, saying, 'Go ye and proclaim the king's victory. The foe hath been routed, and the kine have been recovered.' And the Matsya and the Bharata princes having thus consulted together re-approached the same *Sami* tree. And gratified with the victory they had won, and arrived at the foot of the *Sami* tree, they wore on their persons and took up on their car the ornaments and robes they had left there. And having vanquished the whole hostile army and recovered the whole of the wealth from the Kurus, the heroic son of Virata returned to the city with Vrihannala as his car-driver."

SECTION LXVII

Vaisampayana said, "Having speedily recovered his wealth Virata owning a large army entered his city with a cheerful heart, accompanied by the four Pandavas. And having vanquished the *Trigartas* in battle and recovered all the kine, that mighty monarch, along with the sons of Pritha, looked resplendent and blazed forth in beauty. And as the brave king, that enhancer of the joys of friends, was seated on his throne, all his subjects headed by the Brahmanas stood before him. And worshipped by them, the king of the Matsyas, at the head of his army, saluted the Brahmanas and his subjects in return and dismissed them cheerfully. And Virata, the king of the Matsyas owning a large army, enquired after Uttara, saying, 'Where hath Uttara gone?' And the women and the maidens of the palace and the other females living in the inner apartments joyfully said unto him, 'Our kine having been seized by the Kurus, Bhuminjaya incensed at this and from excess of bravery hath issued forth alone with only Vrihannala as his second, for vanquishing the six mighty car-warriors, Bhishma the son of Santanu, and Kripa, and Karna, and Duryodhana, and Drona, and Drona's son who have all come with the Kuru army.'"

Vaisampayana continued, "Then king Virata, hearing that his brave son had gone forth with only one car and with Vrihannala as his car-driver, became filled with grief, and addressing his chief counsellors, said, 'Without doubt, the Kauravas and other lords of earth, learning the defeat of the Trigartas, will never keep their ground. Therefore, let those of my warriors that have not been wounded by the *Trigartas* go out, accompanied by a mighty force, for the protection of Uttara.' And saying this, the king speedily despatched, for the sake of his son, horses and elephants and cars and a large number of foot-soldiers, equipped and decked with various kinds of weapons and ornaments. And it was thus that Virata, the king of the Matsyas, owning a large army, quickly ordered out a large division consisting of four kinds of troops. And having done this, he said, 'Learn ye, without loss of time whether the prince liveth still or not! I myself think that he who hath got a person of the neuter sex for his car-driver is not alive.'"

Vaisampayana continued, "Then king Yudhishthira the just, smilingly said unto the afflicted king Virata, 'If, O monarch, Vrihannala hath been his charioteer, the foe will never be able to take away thy kine today. Protected by that charioteer, thy son will be able to vanquish in battle all the lords of earth allied with the Kurus, indeed, even the gods and the *Asuras* and the *Siddhas* and the *Yakshas* together.'"

Vaisampayana continued, "Meanwhile, the swift-footed messengers despatched by Uttara, having reached Virata's city, gave tidings of the victory. And the minister-in-chief then informed the king of everything, viz., the great victory that had been won, the defeat of the Kurus, and the expected arrival of Uttara. And he said, 'All the kine have been brought back, the Kurus have been defeated, and Uttara, that slayer of foes, is well with his car-driver.' Then Yudhishthira said, 'By good luck it is that the kine have been recovered and the Kurus routed. I do not, however, regard it strange that thy son should have vanquished the Kurus, for his victory is assured that hath Vrihannala for his charioteer.'"

Vaisampayana continued, "Hearing of the victory of his son possessed of immeasurable might, king Virata became so glad that the bristles of his body stood erect. And having made presents of raiments unto the messengers, he ordered his ministers, saying, 'Let the highways be decorated with flags, and let all the gods and goddesses be worshipped with flowery offerings. And let princes and brave warriors, and musicians and harlots decked in ornaments, march out to receive my son. And let the bellman, speedily riding an intoxicated elephant, proclaim my victory at places where four roads meet. And let Uttara, too, in gorgeous attire and surrounded by virgins and chanters of eulogies, go forth to receive my son.'"

Vaisampayana continued, "Having listened to these words of the king, all the citizens with auspicious things in hand, and many amongst them with cymbals and trumpets and conchs, and beautiful women attired in gorgeous robes, and reciters of auspicious and sacred hymns, accompanied by encomiasts and minstrels, and drummers and other kinds of musicians issued forth from the city of the mighty Virata to welcome Uttara of immeasurable prowess. And having despatched troops and maidens and courtesans decked in ornaments, the wise king of the Matsyas cheerfully said these words, '*O Sairindhri*, fetch the dice. And, O Kanka, let the play commence.' The son of Pandu replied, saying, 'We have heard it said that one whose heart is filled with joy should not play with a cunning gambler. I do not therefore, dare gamble with thee that are so transported with joy. I am ever desirous of doing what is for thy good. Let the play, however, commence if it pleases thee.'

"Virata said, 'My female slaves and kine, my gold and whatsoever other wealth I have, nothing of all this shall thou be able to protect today even if I do not gamble.' Kanka said in reply, 'O monarch, O bestower of honours, what business hast thou with gamble which is attended with numerous evils? Gambling is fraught with many evils; it should, therefore, be shunned. Thou mayst have seen or at least heard of Yudhishthira, the son of Pandu. He lost his extensive and prosperous kingdom and his god-like brothers at dice. For this, I am averse to gambling. But if thou likest, O king, I will play.'"

Vaisampayana continued, "While the play was going on, Matsya said unto the son of Pandu, 'Lo, the Kauravas that are so formidable have been vanquished in battle by my son.' Upon this, the illustrious king Yudhishthira said, 'Why should not he conquer that hath Vrihannala for his charioteer?'

"Thus addressed, King Matsya became angry and said unto Pandu's son, 'Thou wretch of a Brahmana, dost thou compare one of the neuter sex with my son! Hast thou no knowledge of what is proper and what improper for one to say? Without doubt, thou disregardest me. Why should not my son vanquish all those with Bhishma and Drona as their leaders? O Brahmana, for friendship only I pardon thee this thy offence. Thou must not, however, say so again if thou wishest to live.'

"Yudhishthira said, 'There where Bhishma and Drona and Drona's son and the son of Vikartana and Kripa and king Duryodhana and other royal and mighty car-warriors are assembled or there where Indra himself is surrounded by the Maruts, what other person than Vrihannala can fight, encountering them all! None hath been, none will be, his equal in strength of arms! Indeed, it is Vrihannala only whose heart is filled with joy at sight of a terrible conflict. It is he who had vanquished the celestials and the *Asuras* and human beings fighting together. With such a one for his ally, why should not thy son conquer the foe?' Virata said, 'Repeatedly forbidden by me, thou dost not yet restrain thy tongue. If there is none to punish, no one would practise virtue.'"

Vaisampayana continued, "Saying this, the king inflamed with anger forcibly struck Yudhishthira in the face with a dice, and reproached him angrily, saying, 'Let it not occur again!' And having been violently struck, blood began to flow from his nose. But the son of Pritha held it in his hands before it fell on the ground. And the virtuous Yudhishthira then glanced at Draupadi who was standing by his side. Ever obedient to the wishes of her lord, the faultless Draupadi, understanding his meaning, and bringing a golden vessel filled with water, received the blood that flowed from his nose. Meanwhile, Uttara, entertained with sweet perfumes of diverse kinds and decked with floral chaplets, slowly entered the city, received with respect by the citizens, the women, and the people of the provinces. And approaching the gate of the palace he sent the news of his arrival to his father. And the porter then, approaching the king, said, 'Thy son Uttara, waiteth at the gate with Vrihannala as his companion.' And the Matsya king, with a cheerful heart, said unto him, 'Do thou usher both, as I am very anxious to see them.' Then Yudhishthira, the king of the Kurus, gently whispered unto the ears of the warder, 'Let Uttara enter alone; Vrihannala must not come in. Such is the vow of that hero of mighty arms that whoever causeth a wound on my person or sheddeth my blood except in battle, shall not live. Inflamed with rage he will never bear patiently to see me bleeding, but will slay Virata even now with his counsellors and troops and steeds.'"

SECTION LXVIII

Vaisampayana said, "Then Bhuminjaya, the eldest son of the king, entered, and having worshipped the feet of his father approached Kanka. And he beheld Kanka covered with blood, and seated on the ground at one end of the court, and waited upon by the *Sairindhri*. And seeing this, Uttara asked his father in a hurry, saying, 'By whom, O king, hath this one been struck? By whom hath this sinful act been perpetrated?'

"Virata said, 'This crooked Brahmana hath been struck by me. He deserveth even more than this. When I was praising thee, he praised that person of the third sex.'

"Uttara said, 'Thou hast, O king, committed an improper act. Do thou speedily propitiate him so that the virulent poison of a Brahmana's curse may not consume thee to thy roots!'"

Vaisampayana continued, "Having heard the words of his son, Virata, that enhancer of the limits of his kingdom, began to soothe Kunti's son, who was like unto a fire hid in ashes, for obtaining his forgiveness. And unto the king desirous of obtaining his pardon the Pandava replied, 'O king, I have long ago forgiven it. Anger I have none. Had this blood from my nostrils fallen on the ground, then, without doubt, thou, O monarch, wouldst have been destroyed with thy kingdom. I do not, however, blame thee, O king, for having struck an innocent person. For, O king, they that are powerful generally act with unreasoning severity.'"

Vaisampayana continued, "When the bleeding had stopped, Vrihannala entered (the council-room) and having saluted both Virata and Kanka, stood silent. And the king, having appeased the chief of the Kurus, began to praise, in Savyasachin's hearing, Uttara who had returned from the battle. And the king said, 'O enhancer of the joys of Kekaya's princess, in thee have I truly a son! I never had nor shall have, a son that is equal to thee! How, indeed, couldst thou, O child, encounter that Karna who leaveth not a single mark unhit amongst even a thousand that he may aim at all at once? How couldst thou, O child, encounter that Bhishma who hath no equal in the whole world of men? How also couldst thou, O child, encounter Drona, that foremost of all wielders of weapons, that preceptor of the Vrishnis and

Kauravas, twice-born one who may be regarded as the preceptor of all the Kshatriyas? How couldst thou meet in battle the celebrated Aswatthaman? How couldst thou, O child, encounter that Duryodhana, the prince who is capable of piercing even a mountain with his mighty arrows? My foes have all been thrashed. A delicious breeze seems to blow around me. And since thou hast recovered in battle the whole of my wealth that had been seized by the Kurus, it seems that all those mighty warriors were struck with panic. Without doubt, thou, O bull amongst men, has routed the foe and snatched away from them my wealth of kine, like his prey from a tiger.'"

SECTION LXIX

"Uttara said, 'The kine have not been recovered by me, nor have the foe been vanquished by me. All that hath been accomplished by the son of a deity. Capable of striking like a thunderbolt, that youth of celestial origin, beholding me running away in fear, stopped me and himself mounted on my car. It was by him that the kine have been recovered and the Kauravas vanquished. The deed, O father, is that hero's and not mine. It was he that repulsed with arrows Kripa and Drona and Drona's son of powerful energy, and the *Suta's* son and Bhishma. That mighty hero then spoke unto the affrighted prince Duryodhana who was running away like the leader of a head of elephants, these words, "O prince of the Kuru race, I do not see that thou art safe by any means even at Hastinapura. Protect thy life by putting forth thy might. Thou shalt not escape me by flight. Therefore, make up thy mind for fight. If victorious, the sovereignty of the earth will be thine, or if slain, heaven itself will be thine."

"'Thus addressed, king Duryodhana—that tiger among men surrounded by his counsellors,—sighing on his car like a snake turned back, showered arrows endued with the speed and force of thunderbolts. Beholding all this, venerable sire, my thighs began to quake. Then that celestial youth pierced with arrows the Kuru army consisting of leonine warriors. And having pierced and afflicted that crowd of cars, that youth, stout as the lion, laughed at them and robbed them of their clothes and attires. Indeed, the six great car-warriors of the Kurus were vanquished by that hero alone, even like herds of animals ranging in the forest by a single tiger in rage.'

"Virata said, 'Where is that mighty-armed and famous youth of celestial origin, that hero who recovered in battle my wealth that had been seized by the Kurus? I am anxious to behold and worship that mighty warrior of celestial origin who hath saved thee and my kine also.'

"Uttara replied, 'The mighty son of a deity disappeared there and then. I think, however, that he will show himself either tomorrow or the day after.'"

Vaisampayana continued, "Virata, that owner of a large army, remained ignorant of the son of Pandu who was thus described unto him by Uttara, and who was living in the palace in disguise. And permitted by the high-souled Virata, Partha presented with his own hands the garments he had brought, unto Virata's daughter. And the beautiful Uttara, obtaining those new and costly clothes of diverse kinds, became highly glad, along with the son of the Matsya king."

SECTION LXX

Vaisampayana said, "Then, on the third day, attired in white robes after a bath, and decked in ornaments of all kinds, those great car-warriors, the five Pandava brothers, having accomplished their vow, and with Yudhishthira at their head, looked resplendent as they entered the palace-gate like five intoxicated elephants. And having entered the council-hall of Virata, they took their seats on the thrones reserved for kings, and shone brilliantly like fires on the sacrificial altar. And after Pandavas had taken their seats, Virata, that lord of earth, came there for holding his council and discharging other royal offices. And beholding the illustrious Pandavas blazing like fires, the king reflected for a moment. And then, filled with wrath, the Matsya king spoke unto Kanka seated there like a celestial and looking like the lord of celestials surrounded by the Martus. And he said, 'A player at dice thou wert employed by me as a courtier! How couldst thou occupy the royal seat thus attired in handsome robes and ornaments?'"

Vaisampayana continued, "Hearing these words of Virata, O king, and desirous of jesting with him, Arjuna smilingly said in reply, 'This person, O king, deserveth to occupy the same seat with Indra himself. Devoted to the Brahmanas, acquainted with the *Vedas*, indifferent to luxury and carnal enjoyments, habitually performing sacrifices, steady in vows, this one, indeed, is the very embodiment of virtue. The foremost of all Persons endued with energy and superior to every body on earth in intelligence, devoted to asceticism, he is conversant with various weapons. No other person among the mobile and immobile creatures of the three worlds possesseth or will ever possess such knowledge of weapons. And there is none even amongst the gods, or *Asuras*, or men, or *Rakshasas*, or *Gandharvas*, or *Yaksha* chiefs, or *Kinnaras*—or mighty *Uragas*, who is like him. Endued with great foresight and energy, beloved by the citizens and inhabitants of the provinces, he is the mightiest of car-warriors amongst the sons of Pandu. A performer of sacrifices, devoted to morality, and of subdued passions, like unto a great *Rishi*, this royal sage is celebrated over all the worlds. Possessed of great strength and great intelligence, able and truthful, he hath all his senses under complete control. Equal unto Indra in wealth and Kuvera in hoarding, he is the protector of the worlds like unto *Manu* himself of mighty prowess. Endued with great might, he is even such. Kind unto all creatures he is no other than the bull of the Kuru race, king Yudhishthira the just. The achievements of this king resemble the sun himself of blazing effulgence. And his fame hath travelled in all directions like the rays of that luminary. And like the rays following the risen sun of blazing effulgence, ten thousand swift elephants followed him, O king, when he dwelt among the Kurus. And, O king, thirty thousand cars decked in gold and drawn by the best steeds, also used to follow him then. And full eight hundred bards adorned with ear-rings set with shining gems, and accompanied by minstrels, recited his praises in those days, like the *Rishis* adorning Indra. And, O king, the Kauravas and other lords of earth always waited upon him like slaves, as the celestials upon Kuvera. This eminent king, resembling the bright-rayed sun, made all lords of earth pay tribute unto him like persons of the agricultural class. And eighty-eight thousands of high-souled *Snatakas* depended for their subsistence upon this king practising excellent vows. This illustrious lord protected the aged and the helpless, the maimed and the blind, as his sons, and he ruled over his subjects virtuously. Steady in morality and self-control, capable of restraining his anger, bountiful, devoted to the Brahmanas, and truthful, this one is the son of Pandu. The prosperity and prowess of this one afflict king Suyodhana with his followers including Karna and Suvala's son. And, O lord of men, the virtues of this one are incapable of being enumerated. This son of Pandu is devoted to morality and always abstains from injury. Possessed of such attributes, doth not this bull among kings, this son of Pandu, deserve, O monarch, to occupy a royal seat?'"

SECTION LXXI

"Virata said, 'If this one, indeed, be the Kuru king Yudhishthira the son of Kunti, which amongst these is his brother Arjuna, and which, the mighty Bhima. Which of these is Nakula, and which Sahadeva and where is the celebrated Draupadi? After their defeat at dice, the sons of Pritha have not been heard of by any one.'

"Arjuna said, 'Even this one, O king, who is called Vallava and is thy cook, is that Bhima of mighty arms and terrible prowess and furious impetus. It was he who slew the furious *Rakshasas* on the mountains of *Gandhamadana*, and procured for Krishna celestial flowers of great fragrance. Even he is that *Gandharva*, who slew the Kichaka of wicked soul and it was he who killed tigers and bears and boars in the inner apartment of thy palace. He who had been the keeper of thy horse is that slayer of foes called Nakula, and this one is Sahadeva, the keeper of thy kine. Both these sons of Madri are great car-warriors, possessed of great fame and beauty of person. These two bulls of the Bharata race, attired in handsome robes and decked in excellent ornaments, are a match for a thousand great car-warriors. And even this lady of eyes like lotus-petals and slender waist and sweet smiles is Drupada's daughter, thy wife's *Sairindhri*, for whose sake, O king, the Kichakas were slain. I am, O king, Arjuna who, it is evident, thou hast heard, is that son of Pritha, who is Bhima's junior and the senior of the twins! We have, O king, happily passed in thy abode the period of non-discovery, like infants in the womb!'"

Vaisampayana continued, "After Arjuna had pointed out those heroes—the five Pandavas, the son of Virata then spoke of Arjuna's prowess. And Uttara once again identified the sons of Pritha. And the prince said, 'That one whose complexion is bright like that of pure gold, who is stout like a full-grown lion, whose nose is so prominent, whose eyes are large and expansive, and whose face is broad and of coppery hue, is the king of the Kurus. And behold, that one whose tread is like that of an infuriate elephant, whose complexion is like that of heated gold, whose shoulders are broad and expanded, and whose arms are long and thick, is Vrikodara. And he who stands by his side, that youth of darkish hue, who is like unto a leader of a herd of elephants, whose shoulders are broad like those of a lion, whose tread is like that of a mighty elephant, and whose eyes are large and expansive like lotus-leaves, is Arjuna that foremost of bowmen. All lo, close to the king, are those foremost of men, the twins, like unto Vishnu and Indra, and who have no equals, in the world of men, in beauty, might, and behaviour. And close by them, behold, standeth Krishna, beautiful as gold, like unto the very embodiment of light, possessing the complexion of the blue lotus, like unto a celestial damsel, and resembling the living embodiment of *Lakshmi* herself.'"

Vaisampayana continued, "Then Virata's son began to describe the prowess of Arjuna, saying, 'Even this one is he that slew the foe, like unto a lion devastating a flock of deer. Even he ranged through crowds of hostile cars, slaying their best of car-warriors. By him was slain a huge, infuriate elephant by means of a single arrow. Pierced by him, that huge beast having its flanks adorned with an armour of gold, fell down piercing the earth with his tusks. By him have the kine been recovered and the Kauravas vanquished in battle. My ears have been deafened by the blare of his conch. It was by this hero of fierce deeds that Bhishma and Drona, along with Duryodhana, were vanquished. That achievement is his and not mine.'"

Vaisampayana continued, "Hearing these words of his, the mighty king of the Matsyas, considering himself guilty of having offended Yudhishthira, said unto Uttara in reply, 'I think the time hath come for me to propitiate the sons of Pandu. And, if thou likest, I shall bestow my daughter Uttara upon Arjuna.'

"Uttara said, 'Worthy of our adorations and worship and respect, the time hath come for worshipping the illustrious sons of Pandu who deserve to be worshipped by us.'

"Virata said, 'When brought under the foe's subjection in battle, it was Bhimasena that rescued me. My kine also have been recovered by Arjuna. It is through the might of their arms that we have obtained victory in battle. Such being the case, all of us, with our counsellors, shall propitiate Yudhishthira the son of Kunti. Blessed be thou, with all thy brothers, O bull among the sons of Pandu. If, O king, we have ever said or done anything in ignorance to offend thee, it behoveth thee to forgive us. The son of Pandu is virtuous.'"

Vaisampayana continued, "Then the high-souled Virata, delighted greatly, approached king Yudhishthira and made an alliance with him, and offered him his whole kingdom together with the sceptre and treasury and metropolis. And addressing all the Pandavas, and especially Dhananjaya, the mighty king of the Matsyas repeatedly said, 'By good luck it is that I see you.' And having again and again embraced Yudhishthira and Bhima and the sons of Madri, and smelt their heads, Virata, that owner of a large army, was not satiated with gazing at them. And being highly pleased, he said unto king Yudhishthira, 'By good luck it is that I see you safe from woods. By good luck it is that ye have accomplished with difficulty the period of exile, undiscovered by those wicked wights. I make over my entire kingdom to the sons of Pritha, and what else I have. Let the sons of Pandu accept these without the slightest hesitation. And let Dhananjaya, called also Savyasachin, accept the hand of Uttara: for that best of men is fit to be her lord.' Thus addressed, king Yudhishthira the just cast a look upon Dhananjaya, the son of Pritha. And looked at by his brother, Arjuna said unto the Matsya king, 'O monarch, I accept thy daughter as my daughter-in-law. And alliance of this kind between the Matsya and the Bharatas is, indeed, desirable.'"

SECTION LXXII

"Virata said, 'Why, O best among the Pandavas, dost thou not wish to accept as wife this my daughter that I bestow upon thee?'

"Arjuna said, 'Residing in thy inner apartments, I had occasion always to behold thy daughter, and she too, alone or in company trusted me as her father. Well-versed in singing and dancing, I was liked and regarded by her, and, indeed, thy daughter always regardeth me as her protector. O king, I lived for one whole year with her though she had attained the age of puberty. Under these circumstances, thyself or other men may not without reason, entertain suspicions against her or me. Therefore, O king, myself who am pure, and have my senses under control, beg to thee, O monarch, thy daughter as my daughter-in-law. Thus do I attest her purity. There is no difference between a daughter-in-law and a daughter, as also between a son and son's own-self. By adopting this course, therefore, her purity will be proved. I am afraid of slanderous and false accusations. I accept, therefore, O king, thy daughter Uttara as my daughter-in-law. Surpassing all in knowledge of weapons, resembling a celestial youth in beauty, my son, the mighty-armed Abhimanyu is the favourite nephew of Vasudeva, the wielder of the discus. He, O king, is fit to be thy son-in-law and the husband of thy daughter.'

"Virata said, 'It behoveth the best of the Kurus, Dhananjaya, the son of Kunti, who is so virtuous and wise, to say this. O son of Pritha, do thou carry out what thou thinkest should be done after this. He that hath Arjuna for the father of his son-in-law, hath all his desires gratified.'"

Vaisampayana continued, "The monarch having said this, Yudhishthira, the son of Kunti, gave his assent to what was thus agreed upon between the Matsya king and Arjuna. And, O Bharata, the son of Kunti sent invitations to Vasudeva and to all his friends and relatives, and Virata also did the same. And then, after the expiry of the thirteenth year, the five Pandavas took up their abode in one of Virata's towns called *Upaplavya*, and Vibhatsu, the son of Pandu, brought over Abhimanyu and Janardana, and also many people of the Dasarha race from the Anarta country. And the king of Kasi, and also Saivya, being very friendly to Yudhishthira, arrived there, each accompanied by an *Akshauhini* of troops. And the mighty Drupada, also with the heroic sons of Draupadi and the unvanquished Sikhandin, and that foremost of wielder of weapons, the invincible Dhrishtadyumna came there with another *Akshauhini* of troops. And all the kings that came were not only lords of *Akshauhini*, but performers of sacrifices with gifts in profusion to Brahmanas, conversant with the *Vedas* endued with heroism, and ready to die in battle. And beholding them arrived, that foremost of virtuous men, the king of the Matsyas, adored them duly, and entertained their troops and servants and carriers of burdens. And he was highly pleased to bestow his daughter upon Abhimanyu. And after the kings had come there from different parts of the country, there came Vasudeva decked in floral garlands, and Halayudha, and Kritavarman, the son of Hridika, and Yuyudhana, the son of Satyaki, and Anadhristi and Akrura, and Samva and Nisatha. And these repressers of foes came there bringing with them Abhimanyu and his mother. And Indrasena and others, having lived at Dwaraka for one whole year, came there, bringing with them the well adorned cars of the Pandavas. And there came also ten thousand elephants and ten thousand cars, and hundred millions of horses and hundred billions of foot-soldiers, and innumerable Vrishni and Andhaka and Bhoja warriors of great energy, in the train of that tiger among the Vrishnis, Vasudeva of great effulgence. And Krishna gave unto each of the illustrious sons of Pandu numerous female slaves, and gems and robes. And then the nuptial festival set in between the families of the Matsya king and the Pandavas. And then conchs and cymbals and horns and drums and other musical instruments appointed by the Pandavas, began to play in the palace of Virata. And deer of various kinds and clean animals by hundreds were slain. And wines of various kinds and intoxicating juices of trees were profusely collected. And mimes and bards and encomiasts, versed in singing and legendary lore, waited upon the kings, and chanted their praises and genealogies. And the matrons of the Matsyas of symmetrical bodies and limbs, and wearing ear-rings of pearls and gems, headed by Sudeshna, came to the place where the marriage knot was to be tied. And amongst those beautiful females of fair complexion and excellent ornaments, Krishna was the foremost in beauty and fame and splendour. And they all came there, leading forth the princess Uttara decked in every ornament and resembling the daughter of the great Indra himself. And then Dhananjaya, the son of Kunti, accepted Virata's daughter of faultless limbs on behalf of his son by Subhadra. And that great king, Yudhishthira, the son of Kunti, who stood there like Indra, also accepted her as his daughter-in-law. And having accepted her, the son of Pritha, with Janardana before him, caused the nuptial ceremonies to be performed of the illustrious son of Subhadra. And Virata then gave him (as dowry) seven thousand steeds endued with the speed of the wind and two hundred elephants of the best kind and much wealth also. And having duly poured libations of clarified butter on the blazing fire, and paid homage unto the twice-born ones, Virata offered to the Pandavas his kingdom, army, treasury, and his own self. And after the marriage had taken place, Yudhishthira, the son of Dharma, gave away unto the Brahmanas all the wealth that had been brought by Krishna of unfading glory. And he also gave away thousands of kine, and diverse kinds of robes, and various excellent ornaments, and vehicles, and beds, delicious viands of various kinds, and cardinal drinks of diverse species. And the king also made gifts of land unto the Brahmanas with due rites, and also cattle by thousands. And he also gave away thousands of steeds and much gold and much wealth of other kinds, unto persons of all ages. And, O bull of the Bharata race, the city of the Matsya king, thronged with men cheerful and well-fed, shone brightly like a great festival."

Footnote 1:

Brahma Vadini—Nilakantha explains this as *Krishna-kirtanasila.*

Footnote 2:

This speech of Vaisampayana is not included in some texts within the second section. To include it, however, in the third, is evidently a mistake.

Footnote 3:

The sloka commencing with *Adushta* and ending *ratheshu cha* does not occur in texts except those in Bengal.

Footnote 4:

A difference reading is observable here. The sense, however, is the same.

Footnote 5:

An independent female artisan working in another person's house.—Wilson.

Footnote 6:

Some of the Bengal text and *Sarvatramaya* for *Sarvamantramaya*. The former is evidently incorrect.

Footnote 7:

This is a very difficult *sloka*. Nilakantha adopts the reading *Sanjayet*. The Bengal editions read *Sanjapet*. If the latter be the correct reading, the meaning then would be,—'Let none talk about what transpires in the presence of the king. For those even that are poor, regard it as a grave fault.' The sense evidently is that the occurrences in respect of a king which one witnesses should not be divulged. Even they that are powerless regard such divulgence of what occurs in respect of them as an insult to them, and, therefore, inexcusable.

Footnote 8:

The Bengal editions read *Rajna* in the instrumental case. Following a manuscript text of a Pandit of my acquaintance I read *Rajnas* in the genitive.

Footnote 9:

Mahishasura, the son of Rambhasura. Durga had to fight for many years before she could slay this formidable *Asura*. The story occurs in the *Markandeya Purana*. To this day, Bengal during the great Durga Puja festival in autumn, worships the goddess with great veneration.

Footnote 10:

Literally, one that rescues from difficulty.

Footnote 11:

Kamachara is explained by Nilakantha thus, although in other places it bears a quite different meaning.

Footnote 12:

Krita—attack; *Pratikrita*—warding it off; *Sankata*—clenched. *Some* texts read *Sankatakais*. The meaning then would be 'cased in gauntlets.'

Footnote 13:

Bhuti, Hri, Sri, Kirti and *Kanti* are respectively the feminine embodiments of Prosperity, Modesty, Beauty, Fame and Loveliness.

Footnote 14:

What Draupadi means is that instead of passing her days in joy and happiness, instead of being able to wish time to be stationary with her, she is obliged in consequence of her misery, to wish time to pass off quickly.

Footnote 15:

Jayate asyas—i.e., she from whom one is born.

Footnote 16:

Some texts read, *Vilwam nagaviodhara—i.e.,* 'As an elephant lifts up a vela fruit.'

Footnote 17:

Weri means both a kettle-drum and a trumpet. The latter however conveys a better meaning here.

Footnote 18:

Literature, force of his thighs.

Footnote 19:

What Bhima says is this.—The Gandharvas, your husbands, are always obedient to thee! If they have been able to do thee a service, they have only repaid a debt.

Footnote 20:

Krita-krita—Nilakantha explains this to mean 'imagining themselves to have achieved success in their mission' for having learnt of Kichaka's death, they could readily guess the presence of the Pandavas there. This is too far-fetched and does not at all agree with the spirit of their report to Duryodhana below. And then the same word occurs in the very last line of the Section. I take it that in both places the word has been used in the same sense.

Footnote 21:

This is a very difficult sloka. I am not sure that I have understood it alright. Both Nilakantha and Arjuna Misra are silent. Instead of depending, however, on my own intelligence, I have consulted several friends who have read the *Mahabharata* thoroughly. The grammatical structure is easy. The only difficulty consists in the second half of the sloka. The meaning, however, I have given is consistent with the tenor of Bhishma's advice.

Footnote 22:

Indicating the unobstructed completion of the sacrifice.

Footnote 23:

The word *tirtha* here means, as Nilakantha rightly explains spies and not holy spots.

Footnote 24:

Satram is explained by Nilakantha to mean here 'false disguise.' I think, however, such an interpretation to be far-fetched. It evidently means 'forest',—the use of 'pravisteshu' in connection with it almost settles the point.

Footnote 25:

This sloka is not correctly printed in any of the texts that I have seen. The reading that I adopt is that the second word is the participle of the root *budh* and not the instrumental of *budhi*; the last word again of the second line is a compound of *valavatsu* and *avaleshu* instead of (as printed in many books) *valavatswavaleshu*. Any other reading would certainly be incorrect. I have not consulted the Bombay text.

Footnote 26:

Bhagasas lit., each in its proper place. It may also mean, 'according to their respective division.'

Footnote 27:

Kalyana-patalam is explained by Nilakantha to mean *suvarna-pattachchaditam*.

Footnote 28:

One of the generals of Virata.

Footnote 29:

Some differences of reading are noticeable here, for *Yasaswinau* some texts read *Manaswinau*, and for Vahusamravdhau-Vahusanrambhat; and for Nakha-naki—Ratha-rathi.

Footnote 30:

Some texts read Ghanabiva for Ghanarva. The latter is unquestionably better in form.

Footnote 31:

The word in the original is Muhurta equal to 48 minutes. Nilakantha points out very ingeniously that the night being the seventh of the dark fortnight, the moon would not rise till after 14 Dandas from the hour of sunset, a Danda being equal to 24 minutes. A Muhurta, therefore implies not 48 minutes exactly, but some time.

Footnote 32:

Some Vikshyainam, Nilakantha explains Sama as a word spoken by Bhima for assuring the captive Virata, and Vikshya as 'assuring' or 'consoling by a glance.' Perhaps this is right.

Footnote 33:

The adjective Bhima-sankasas as explained by Nilakantha is in this sense, quoting the celebrated simile of Valmiki.

Footnote 34:

To understand the comparison would require in the reader a knowledge of the mechanism of the Indian Vina. Briefly, the Vina consists of a bamboo of about two cubits attached to two gourds towards its ends. Along the bamboo which serves the purpose of a finger-board, is the main chord and several thinner wires. All these pass over a number of frets, two and a half heptachords, representing the total compass of the instrument. The wires rest towards their ends on two pieces of ivory called Upadhanas in Sanskrit or Swaris in Urdu.

Footnote 35:

Some read *kaniasi* for *vaviasi*. Both words are the same, and mean the same thing.

Footnote 36:

Vedi-Vilagnamadhya—Vedi in this connection means a wasp and not, as explained by Mallinatha in his commentary of the *Kumarasambhava,* a sacrificial platform. I would remark in passing that many of the most poetic and striking adjectives in both the Raghu and the *Kumarasambhava* of Kalidasa are borrowed unblushingly from the *Ramayana* and the *Mahabharata*.

Footnote 37:

Padma patrabha-nibha may also mean 'of the splendour of the gem called Marakata.' Nilakantha, however, shows that this would militate against the adjective *Kankojwalatwacham* below.

Footnote 38:

The princess being of the complexion of burnished gold and Arjuna dark as a mass of clouds, the comparison is exceedingly appropriate. The Vaishnava poets of Bengal never tire of this simile in speaking of Radha and Krishna in the groves of Vrindavana.

Footnote 39:

The words in the original is *pranayam,* lit., love. Nilakantha, however, explains it as meaning modesty, humility. I think, Nilakantha is right. The relations between Arjuna and the princess were like those between father and daughter.

Footnote 40:

This sloka is not correctly printed in any of the texts that I have seen. The Burdwan Pandits read *tat-samim*. This I think, is correct, but then *asasada* in the singular when the other verbs are all dual seems to be correct. The poet must have used some other verb in the dual for *asasada*.

Footnote 41:

Some texts read *Diptasya* for *Diptayam*.

Footnote 42:

This sloka does not occur in every text. This is a typical illustration of the round about way, frequently adopted by Sanskrit writers, of expressing a simple truth. The excuse in the present instance consists in Drona's unwillingness to identify the solitary hero with Arjuna, in the midst of all his hearers. Nadiji is an exclamation referring to Bhishma, the son of the river Ganga. *Lankesa-vanari-ketu* is simply 'ape-bannered,' or as rendered in the text, having the devastator of the gardens of Lanka's lord for the sign of his banner. Nagahvaya is 'named after tree' for Arjuna is the name of an Indian tree. Nagri-sunu is 'Indra's son',—Indra being the foe of mountain, for formerly it was he who cut off the wings of all mountains and compelled them to be stationary. He failed only in the case of Mainaka, the son of Himavat.

Footnote 43:

Indian insects of a particular kind.

Footnote 44:

Most editions read *chapas* which is evidently wrong. The correct reading is *avapas,* meaning quiver. The Burdwan Pandits give this latter reading.

Footnote 45:

Some read *chandrargha-darsanas*. The correct reading is *chandrardha-darsanas*.

Footnote 46:

Most editions read *hema-punkha* and *silasita* in the instrumental plural; the correct reading is their nominative plural forms.

Footnote 47:

Sayaka means here, as explained by Nilakantha, a sword, and not a shaft.

Footnote 48:

From the colour of his steeds.

Footnote 49:

Nilakantha spends much learning and ingenuity in making out that sixty-five years in this connection means thirty-two years of ordinary human computation.

Footnote 50:

Some texts read,—'One large meteor fell.'

Footnote 51:

In some editions read,—*Bharata dwijam,* and *Maha-hardam* for *maha-drumam*. The meaning would then be,—'The banners (of the hostile army) began to tremble in the sky, and large lakes were agitated.'

Footnote 52:

Some texts read *Maharatham* (incorrectly) for *hiranmayan*. Indeed, *Maharatham* would give no meaning in this connection. The incomplete edition of the Roy Press under the auspices of the Principal of the Calcutta Sanskrit College abounds with such incorrect readings and misprints.

Footnote 53:

The Roy Press edition adds here a line which looks very much like an interpolation.

Footnote 54:

The true reading is *Acharya* in the dual number, meaning Drona and Kripa. Some texts read the word in the singular form. Nilakantha notices both these reading, but prefers the dual to the singular.

Footnote 55:

The meaning is rather doubtful. Duryodhana seems to say that 'the hostile appearance of Arjuna has been an act of imprudence on his part. The Pandavas, after the expiry of the thirteenth year, would claim their kingdom. I, Duryodhana, may or may not accede to their demand. When, therefore, it was not certain that Arjuna would be refused by me, his hostile appearance is unwise. He has come sure of victory, but he may yet be defeated.'

Footnote 56:

The sense seems to be that when moralists even are puzzled in judging of the propriety or otherwise of their acts, it can easily be imagined that the Pandavas, however virtuous, have, in the matter of this their appearance, acted wrongly, for, after all, the thirteenth year may not have really been over as believed by them. Or, it may mean, that as regards our presence here, we have not acted imprudently when even moralists cannot always arrive at right conclusion. It seems that for this Duryodhana proceeds to justify that presence in the following sentences.